RICHARD SEDDO̶̶̶̶̶̶̶̶̶
(philosophy, ethics, logic and psychology) with Bertrand Russell and John Wisdom — an advocate and colleague of Ludwig Wittgenstein — at Cambridge. He spent his working life as a personnel manager. A student of anthroposophy for seven decades, he is the author of several books including *Mani, His Life and Work, The Future of Humanity, Philosophy as an Approach to the Spirit, Europa* and *The Mystery of Arthur at Tintagel.*

THE CHALLENGE OF LAZARUS–JOHN

An Esoteric Interpretation

Richard Seddon

TEMPLE LODGE

Published in 2015 by Temple Lodge Publishing,
Hillside House, The Square
Forest Row, RH18 5ES

E-mail: office@templelodge.com

www.templelodge.com

A catalogue record for this book is available from the British Library

ISBN 978 1 906999 72 8

Cover by Morgan Creative featuring part of *The Tribute Money* by Masaccio
Typeset by DP Photosetting, Neath, West Glamorgan
Printed and bound by 4edge Limited, Essex, UK

Contents

PART TWO

Preface

It is with considerable temerity that one who has had no schol-
arly background in theology nor is learned in classical Greek
must approach this, the most profound of the Gospels. But a
foundation in philosophy at Cambridge University and a lifelong
study of anthroposophy (spiritual science) may bring a new light
to bear on it, illuminating aspects lost in a long tradition of
commentary. This is only the start of a long road.

From John the Evangelist's many references to the Old Testament, it is clear that he was brought up in the Judaic tradition. He
sometimes adds a remark 'that the scripture be fulfilled' or
'scripture cannot be broken'; this is intelligible only on the
premise that prophets such as Isaiah or the Psalmist were open to
receive prevision of future events. This book is similarly based on
the conviction that Rudolf Steiner too had an extremely accurate
vision of spiritual events. He made no claim to divine inspiration, but has described — in his book *How to Know Higher Worlds*
and elsewhere — how through vigorous discipline of soul the
capacity for spiritual research may today be acquired by means
of new forces brought to earth by Christ himself.

As well as two major lecture cycles on this Gospel, given in
Hamburg and Kassel, Steiner spoke on particular aspects of it in
other cities of central Europe and, in his general lecturing,
especially during 1906-8, he also frequently referred to it.
Moreover, since he experienced the Gospel itself as a path of
initiation, parallels can sometimes be drawn with his other work.
It therefore seemed both feasible and perhaps helpful to draw
together such interpretations in a form that would supplement
existing commentaries from a fresh point of view. However he
also said clearly that 'this Gospel contains material to understand
which one needs to rise to spiritland, which will not be generally
achieved for millennia to come'. The author can only work from
Steiner's recorded remarks as best he may.

The commentary is based on précis of English translations of works by Rudolf Steiner. But readers need to be constantly aware that quotations are taken out of one context and placed into another, which may change their meaning in unintended ways. Nevertheless the overview may have its own value.

Since this book is written primarily for students of anthroposophy, technical terms which Rudolf Steiner developed for spiritual entities — such as etheric and astral body, Life Spirit, Sun evolution — are retained. They are adequately defined in his lecture cycles on this Gospel, and in his book *Occult Science* (recently published as *Esoteric Science*). When quoting the Gospel text he sometimes amends or expands only the point he is explaining, picking up other aspects on other occasions.

The Gospel text is based on the literal interlinear translation by Alfred Marshall[*] (1958) of the Nestlé Greek text. But changes have been made (a) to take account of Rudolf Steiner's interpretation of specific passages, (b) where alternative readings of the Greek suggested by the specialist commentaries of B. Lindars and F. Rittelmeyer[†] are preferred, (c) to ease the flow of English, and (d) where different Greek words are commonly translated by a single English word. The Evangelist's use of the present tense is followed. So is his use of 'belief into' (translated 'inly') rather than 'belief in', because it refers to a real active force for the earth's future and develops into faith, trust and action rather than mere acceptance of an idea. Section headings are inserted by the editor only for convenience of reference.

Whereas ancient languages indicated the first person singular by conjugation, around the time of Christ the word *ego* began to be added. It is ascribed to Jesus between seven and ten times in each Synoptic Gospel, but over 110 times by John. This must be significant, but standard translations give no sign of whether it is used or not. Here it is shown as 'I', which makes it visible. Its use often points not just to Jesus but to the

---

[*] Alfred Marshall, *The RSV Interlinear Greek-English New Testament*, Samuel Bagster and Sons, London 1958.

[†] Barnabas Lindars, *The Gospel of John*, in the series New Century Bible Commentary, Oliphants, London 1972.

Friedrich Rittlemeyer, *Das Johannesevangelium*, Urachhaus, Stuttgart 1938 (1999).

higher self or 'I' which Christ has brought to all mankind who 'believe him inly'.

The Gospel is taken just as it is presented, square brackets [ ] indicating words of questioned authenticity. Comparisons with the Synoptic Gospels are instanced primarily from Mark, which is often thought to be earlier than Matthew or Luke. No attention is paid to sources, possible changes of sequence or successive stages of compilation, discussions of which are readily available if required. The result is not a finished treatise but primarily a stimulus for further study, where each student can craft his own understanding.

I owe particular thanks to Dr Jean Brown and Gil McHattie for their very helpful comments on my draft text, and especially to Sharman Wagstaff for her care in word processing and her patience with the innumerable corrections that have resulted from my continued reading and slowly growing understanding of this important subject.

It has been with astonishment that this Gospel has revealed its great symphonic themes through Rudolf Steiner's words.

Introduction

The Evangelist

The author of the fourth Gospel is clearly identified at 21:24. 'This is the disciple witnessing these things and having written these things, and we know that his witness is true.' The reference is to 'the disciple whom Jesus loved, who also at supper leaned on his breast and said, Lord, who is betraying you?' (21:20). He is not however named anywhere in the Gospel.

The words 'whom Jesus loved' are remarkable. Did he not love each of the Twelve who had stood by him for three years, even Judas? Indeed, did he not love all human beings? These words must have some special meaning. And in the mysteries, 'to indicate that some disciple was the most deeply initiated, it was said that the master loved him' (23.5.08). Which of the disciples was an initiate?

This directs attention uniquely to Lazarus, whose 'raising from the dead' is placed at the very centre of the Gospel. To anyone acquainted with the ancient mysteries this is quite clearly an initiation accomplished by Jesus Christ himself, which lasted the usual three and a half days: 'it is the fourth day' (11:39). Moreover the description is carefully prepared by images of self-development (ch. 10). The body did not suffer decay (hence 'he is sleeping'); and the words 'Come forth' and 'Let him go' (11:43–4) were always used to end an initiation. Thus the Evangelist was an actual initiate, an 'awakened one'. He had seen heaven open, and had exact knowledge of both the soul world and the spiritual world. The sacred name from the Greek mysteries, *Ioannes* (John) would be given after his initiation. Since IOA is the root of the Hebrew name for God (Je-ho-vah) it is understandable that he would not wish to use it in his Gospel, especially to avoid confusion with the Baptist, and in the context of Jesus Christ.

We are told that Jesus already loved Lazarus (11:5), and after his initiation he would be even more worthy of love as the leading individuality who would carry his message to the world. Who Lazarus was has been much debated. But since the discovery of the secret addition to Mark's Gospel (p. 79) it is clear that he was a rich young man, whom we may probably identify with the rich man whom Jesus already loved (Mark 10:21, the young man of Matt. 19:21 and the ruler of Luke 18:22), who was advised to give up 'all that he had' to follow Jesus. From his many scriptural quotations he was clearly well educated in Hebrew tradition and practices, and specialists affirm that he wrote good classical Greek, although his vocabulary suggests that his mother tongue was Aramaic (like that of Jesus). Such a man might well be known to the high priest (18:15). Having given up not only his material wealth but also the 'wealth' of the rigid law and of his lower ego, he would be open to be taught by Jesus and receive initiation from him.

Jesus was accompanied when he raised Lazarus by the Twelve (11:16), as had always been the case in the mysteries, to sustain the forces from the zodiac. So it is not surprising that at the Last Supper they allowed him, rather than Peter, to lie 'in the lap of Jesus' (13:23). Thus he actually experienced Christ's teaching, whereas the other evangelists only knew it by clairvoyance or tradition. He is the only male disciple mentioned at the foot of the cross, despite the fact that the Jews sought to kill him too (12:10). There he is entrusted with 'the mother of Jesus', which in the context of 19:27 means the wisdom that gives his Gospel its unique power.

The friendly rivalry with Peter, which must have been felt at the Last Supper, would be enhanced at the court of Annas when Peter was in temporary denial, and after the Resurrection. This gains archetypal form when Peter is enjoined three times to 'feed my sheep', whereas his enquiry about the beloved disciple is rebuffed with the words 'What is that to you?' (21:21). Here we see the origin of the historical polarity between the immediate task of the Petrine church and the hitherto latent task of the true Christians of St John to 'lead the sheep out to find pasture' (10:9) in the spiritual world, which the churches have presumed to condemn as heretical.

Under threat from the Jews (12:10), it is likely that John was either arrested, persecuted and exiled to Ephesus or escaped. (The John called 'an unschooled, ordinary man' in Acts 4:13 is probably John Zebedee). Once there, we may be confident that he prepares to write his Gospel, especially for the Greeks (translating Hebrew terms). Ephesus is on the coast of Asia Minor, in the orbit of ancient Persia, but essentially a part of Greek culture and a major mystery centre of Artemis/Diana until burnt down in 356 BC. 'These mysteries were long centred on spiritual experience of the Logos, the creative Word, as experienced both in human speech and in natural creation' (2.12.23). Their tradition must have still had some life when John arrived, and we may suppose that he withdrew to study it, without further initiation, as the best vehicle through which to spread the gospel among the Greeks. Paul visited Ephesus twice, in AD 48 and 52, spending more than two years there (Acts 19:10). Is it not likely that John passed to Paul the wisdom he had gained from his initiation and life with Jesus (in exchange for Paul's own experience on the road to Damascus), as the basis for the esoteric school Paul founded at Athens (though external history does not know this) which continued to bear the name of Dionysius the Areopagite?

Specialists are divided as to whether the Gospel was written in the 60s or 80s and perhaps finished later still. Sadducees are not mentioned, and the Pharisees had taken over about AD 70. John is also the author of the Apocalypse or Book of Revelation, which was written on the island of Patmos (Rev. 1:9) about 70 miles from Ephesus, and has a repeated sevenfold structure similar to that of the Gospel. Towards the end of his life he also wrote the three Letters of John to his 'children' (1 John 2:1) in trenchant terms, guarding particularly against the danger of Docetism and its idea of a discarnate Christ. Steiner is reported to have said privately that John wrote the Gospel at the age of 95 and lived to 106.

After a number of short incarnations as martyr, he reincarnated as Christian Rosencreuz and was numbered among the Masters. He can look back on earlier lives that include the Golden King among the Magi, Hosea and Hiram Abif. (If the Golden King died soon after visiting the infant Jesus, and was (exceptionally) reborn a few years later, he would at the Crucifixion be a youth in his twenties.)

The Gospel

We must first be clear that none of the Gospels (*Ev-angel*, inspiration from above) were ever intended as biographies of Jesus in the modern sense. Each seeks firstly to describe the typical soul life of a Christian initiate, a son of God, as understood in the mystery school to which the writer belonged, and only secondly to show how Jesus Christ fulfilled that ideal in his life. We are dealing both with symbols of the soul world and with outer physical reality. That is why the emphasis differs, and why we need all four. John especially turns attention to the most exalted Power working on earth, the pure Sun Logos, which came right down to earth through the instrumentality of Jesus. He draws on powers from the realm of the wisdom-filled Cherubim, which evoke the feeling of the soaring eagle as his symbol. The benefits of the mystery elite are to become available to all.

In seeking to understand these mighty communications, we feel overpowered by their spiritual grandeur; the spiritual greatness of a cosmic being related to humanity sinks into our soul. 'Whereas the synoptics speak of Jesus of Nazareth, this Gospel is really about Christ' (3.2.07). Hence it cannot be explained by the others. We have a picture of the Divine Man, of the spiritual soul of Christ, even his great transcendental ideas. If we receive in reverence what streams from the mighty figure here described, the Christ of the mysteries can come to life within us. And Christ is life! The truths of this Gospel can regenerate the soul in the depths of our being, so that our life body, nourished by this experience of Christ, takes up the life forces – the living water, the bread of life – that will maintain the physical body into the future. It is thus the Gospel of the Being of Christ.

This Gospel is therefore not a textbook written for the intellect. Our intellectual understanding needs to condense into feelings and inner experiences. But it cannot be understood without rising to higher worlds. When used for meditation, as it was in the early days of Christianity, it is an introduction to Christian schooling of the soul and spirit, derived from an initiation by Christ himself. Life and light become a trinity through the bringing of love.

This was therefore the document for all Christian mystics, who strove to mould their lives on the descriptions here given of the personality and being of Jesus Christ; and equally it was for the Christian brotherhoods engaged in practical esotericism, such as the Manichaeans, the Brothers of St John, the Templars, Albigenses, Cathars and Rosicrucians. In a sense the legends of the Grail, Parzival and Lohengrin were a popular expression of their teachings. Whereas the pictures arising from Imagination are less distinct than those of the synoptics, what is based on Inspiration and Intuition stands out most clearly in John as a result of his initiation.

'We should value this Gospel more highly than anything else; but we must penetrate—as spiritual science does—to its spiritual content. We then find the highest which human understanding can gradually attain, a feeling for the infinite' (1.9.10). An immediate life, a feeling of certainty, flows from it. There is no wisdom accessible to man that is not in some way contained in this Gospel. Such a book must however be transformed to meet human needs, which change from age to age.

An outstanding feature is John's grasp of the ego-consciousness newly brought by Christ, which despite the danger of descent into egoism is yet the ground for the higher self 'born from above'. 'One who makes known the great impulses of this Gospel, and orders his life so that everything may be approved by the Being described, creates something in his astral body which during the night permeates it with spiritual content that transforms it to Spirit Self' (30.6.08). In the seven great 'I am' statements, the 'I' manifests in the astral body as a member of the spiritual world, whence it receives forces raying out on all sides to infinity. We thus have an incomparable ladder to the spiritual world for every 'I'.

It is said that John ignores the Transfiguration and the Eucharistic meal. He does however describe an initiation in which Lazarus awakens to the spirit, whereas the Transfiguration is only an Imaginative experience. And he does lead to inner experiences of 'I am the bread of life' and 'I am the true vine', though not to liturgical practice. This points again to the distinct tasks of Peter and of John.

For those who require an outer symbol to accomplish a spiritual act, the union with Christ, the sacrament of Communion will be the way—until their inner strength is powerful enough to unite with Christ without the outer physical medium. Since meditation is so difficult under modern conditions, other methods must also be used. Today the mission of raising Christianity into spiritual wisdom lies with anthroposophy, which is still only at the beginning of its activity. But if one is to succeed, it is from penetrating through to the spiritual substance of this Gospel above all that one must start.

'If someone takes up this Gospel and reads a mere three lines of it, that is of immense consequence to the whole universe; for if no one were to read it, the whole mission of the earth could not be fulfilled. From such activities can stream forth spiritually the forces which add new life to the earth' (24.3.13).

PART ONE

Prelude

The Gospel opens with a meditation on the origin of both world and mankind, not in some mechanical explosion but in a creative deed of the Godhead that gradually condenses out of the spirit. These words contain the eternal truths lying at the foundation of the great world religions, as well as those in the first twelve chapters.

1:1–5 The Word was with God—The Life and the Light of Men

En archē ēn o logos kai o logos ēn pros ton theon kai theos ēn o logos outos ēn en archē pros ton theon panta di autou egeneto kai chōris autŏu egeneto oude en o gegonen en autō zōē ēn kai ē zōē ēn to phōs tōn anthrōpōn kai to phōs en tē skotia phainei kai ē skotia auto ou katelaben

1 Out of the primal forces was the Word, and the Word was with God, and the Word was [a] God. **2** The same was in primal origin towards God. **3** All things became through him, and without him nothing became which has become. **4** In him was Life; and the Life was the Light of men. **5** And the Light shone in the darkness, and the darkness did not take it in.

This is not an abstract 'beginning', but a further development of the primal forces of warmth, gaseous and fluid conditions already created by the Father through the successive Saturn, Sun and Moon evolutions, as described by Rudolf Steiner in his *Esoteric Science*. 'John states quite clearly that the Logos, not the Father, is the creator principle of "all things" in Earth evolution (including humanity). One cannot take the Gospel literally and maintain at the same time that the creator of things visible is the Father God and not the Christ. It then becomes clear how Christ was able to enter the body (the bread) and the blood (the wine). This was understood by the Church Father up to the fourth century' (3.6.21). This expresses Aristotle's distinction between substance and form.

The concept 'Word' already foresees the highest achievement of mankind, the outer expression of inner spiritual content. This Word, spoken into Akashic substance, was conceived by the Evangelist as the non-spatial seed of the human body. It is of macrocosmic stature, an aspect of the Trinity above all Hier-archies of spirit, and had already been presented in all the ancient mysteries — in Greece as *Logos* and Son of God. But the Hebrew concept of Wisdom (Prov. 8:22), that translates as *Sophia* (Greek) or *Spiritus Sanctus* (Holy Spirit) is not the same.

The word usually translated 'beginning' (*archē*) actually identifies the hierarchy of Archai, Spirits of Time (of Personality), whose creation out of eternity was the beginning of time itself. So it is meaningless to ask what went 'before' them. The word *pros* is ambivalent: the Word was first inward, 'with' God (whereas in Genesis 1:3 the Light is already outward, after the separation of sun and earth). But *pros* may also mean 'towards'. For 'from the very origin of planetary existence, the human seed and God faced each other' (30.3.06); otherwise man could never be created as a free being. Only after the Resurrection does the Word 'sit at the right hand of God' (Mark 16:19). One might imagine the out-pouring of creative breath by the Godhead being given form by the Logos as in a larynx, so that all was formed through (*sic*) him.

Forces of Light first worked from the sun, whose spiritual part is the warm love of the Godhead, streaming into the darkness of the inner human being to form us. 'Had it not always shone, the germ of the ego could not possibly have come into existence' (22.5.08). We still do not see light itself, only its reflection from the darkness which has not taken it in — we do not comprehend it in reality. But today Michael can as an Archai give us the new light that shines within us.

1:6–14 *The Word Became Flesh. Children of God*

6 [A] Man came to be, sent from God, named John; **7** this one came as witness, to testify to the Light, that all might believe through him. **8** He was not that Light, but was to testify concerning the Light. **9** The true Light, that gives light to every man, was to come into the world. **10** He was in the world, and the world came to be through him, and the world did not know him. **11** He came into individualities, and the individuals did not receive him. **12** But to all who did receive him, he gave the power to manifest as children of God: to those trusting in his name, **13** who were born, not of bloods, nor of the will of the flesh, nor of human will, but of God. **14** And the Word became flesh, and tabernacled among us, and we beheld his splendour, splendour as of a one-begotten from a father, full of devotion and truth.

The original text was not punctuated, nor were the words even separated; and it had no indefinite article. 'Man' (*anthropos*) is to be taken in the original sense defined by Paul (1 Thess. 5:23) as the whole being of body, soul *and* spirit, which is cosmic, and active also in sleep and between death and rebirth.

The bodily archetype or 'phantom' of the human being, expressed cosmically in the constellations (consonants) and planets (vowels), was known in Hebrew as 'Adam Kadmon', in Scandinavia as 'Ymir'. It 'had already been created on Old Saturn, and modified successively on Sun and Moon by the cosmic forces of Eagle, Lion and Bull, before being harmonized on Earth by those of Waterman. Into this descended the true Light (v. 9) or Elohim, Spirits of Form, who shaped it "in the image and likeness of God, male-and-female"' or hermaphrodite (Gen. 1:27). There is no distinction of sex in spiritland. These were the 'own things' of the true Light, one-begotten as group souls. From this came the soul of the Luke Jesus child.

Then came the Fall, loss of power to conceive asexual mankind, and the gift of the breath of life (Gen. 2:7) to individuals or 'his own people' who were 'born of bloods, of the will of the flesh'. Gradually the Word, the Being of Christ, approached his descent to earth, becoming visible only to children of God, initiates, who received him. He was seen by Zarathustra as Ahura Mazda, by Egyptian priests as Horus, by Moses in the burning bush, by Greeks as Apollo. Finally he 'became flesh' in Jesus of Nazareth.

The 'Light of men' was not outer sunlight but the inner radiance of the astral body. 'The same force which today the eye receives from outside then streamed outwards from us to illuminate objects for the Godhead' (31.10.05). The word truth (*aletheia*) means 'beyond Lethe', that is, in the spirit; and devotion (*charitos*), points to deeds of creative moral imagination inspired in union with the Godhead.*

These first 14 verses, and the first five especially, were written not for information but for individual meditation, and hundreds of people have in past ages done this for a quarter to half an hour every morning, not speculating but absorbing their power. But this is very difficult amid modern life, so an alternative path is given in anthroposophy, which begins in devotion and truth.

---

*See full discussion in *Becoming Aware of the Logos* by Georg Kühlewind, Lindisfarne Press, 1985.

The Baptist's Witness

It is clear from vv. 15,19,32 that this section originates from the Baptist, who also speaks in chapter 3, and indeed this is not retracted until 10:41. His objective was to inaugurate the tremendous change resulting from the Word becoming flesh (v. 14). Jesus confirms that the Baptist had been Elijah (Matt. 11:14, 17:12), 'who had proclaimed a Divinity external to the human being; but the Baptist denied this because he knew that his task was to proclaim that the ego can now find the divine within itself' (2.5.12).

The Word was a God (1:1).

1:15-18 The Fullness—Seeing God

15 John bears witness of him, and proclaimed: This was he of whom I said, The one coming after me has become prior to me, because he was before me. **16** Because of his Fullness we all received, and grace instead of grace; **17** [for the law was given through Moses, grace and truth came to be through Jesus Christ]. **18** No one has ever seen God; the one-begotten [God], being into the lap of the Father, he divulged him.

The Fullness refers to the six Elohim (Exusiai, Spirits of Form) who with Jehovah work as a unity on the human ego—hence we later encounter the sevenfold 'I am'. The Word is a living incarnation of these, but at macrocosmic level. That is the great Sun Being, the true Light constantly ascending and descending, radiating through physical and etheric bodies from higher and lower spiritland respectively.

The Baptist was indeed older than Jesus (Luke 1:41), but the Word was present from the beginning (1:1). He expresses the whole significance of the descent of the Word in his contrast between the old grace of deeds performed in accordance with the law of Moses (actually given by Christ during his descent as the fire in the burning bush) (Exod. 3:2) and deeds based on the soul's capacity to act rightly out of the inner self from moral intuition and the love of goodness for its own sake. When the inmost soul comes alive, 'able to reach the light by its own efforts whilst feeling completely at peace with others and inflamed by love, that is the new grace, a most profound conception of Christianity' (17.3.07).

Although no ordinary person (*oudeis*) has seen God, that did not preclude initiates from doing so as an inner experience (e.g. Jacob, Gen. 32:30). 'The pure in heart shall see God' (Matt. 5:8). But Christ revealed God even for physical experience through his descent into Jesus of Nazareth, who was a human being (although raised to the third degree before his ego withdrew sacrificially to make way for the Logos).

'At the time of the Baptism, all the 'ash' content from the past was removed from the special body of Jesus Christ, so that only the soluble "salt" content, which relates to the cosmos, remained' (12.10.11).

1:19–28 Baptism by John — The Lord in Solitude of Soul

19 This is the testimony of John, when the Jews sent priests and Levites to him from Jerusalem to ask him, Who are you? **20** He confessed and did not deny, and acknowledged: 'I' am not the Christ. **21** They asked him, What then? Are you Elijah? I'm not. Are you the prophet? No. **22** Who then are you, that we may reply to those who sent us — what do you say of yourself? **23** He said, 'I', a voice of calling in the solitude, Make open the way of the lord, as said Isaiah the prophet. **24** Those sent were of the Pharisees, **25** who asked, Why then do you baptize, if you are not the Christ, nor Elijah, nor the prophet? **26** John replied, 'I' baptize in water; but among you stands one whom you do not know, **27** who comes after me, the strap of whose sandal 'I' am not worthy to loosen. **28** These things happened in Bethany beyond the Jordan, where John was baptizing.

The Baptist is of angelic stature (Mark 1:2, *aggelos*); and having been Elijah, the group soul of the Hebrew people, he could already say 'I' (v. 23). Moreover 'his ego had been withheld from the soul of the Luke Jesus at the Fall. Then he had been intimately acquainted with Jesus in the mother-lodge of humanity on the sun. And subsequently he was developed further by the spiritualized body of Buddha preaching compassion and love' (19/ 20.9.09). Now lonely because he was newly separated from the group ego and bloodstream, he saw himself as a voice calling in the solitude (*sic*) of the consciousness soul. His message was clear (Matt. 3, Luke 3): 'Do not rely on Abraham. The tree (of heredity) is cut off at the root; the threshing-floor (of sense perception) is cleared; repent (change your mind-set); for the son of man (p. 32) is here that all shall see; make way for the ('I' as) lord (of the soul forces), gather its fruits into the granary of your soul.'

The rite of baptism practised by John was one of total immersion under water, sufficient to cause in the head a partial deathlike separation of the etheric body from the physical. This was a Waterman initiation, an experience of the Nazarene (Essene) training, but less than the traditional initiation of three and a half days and closer to what the law required for the purification of proselytes. It is neither possible nor necessary today. It enabled not only the life tableau but also images of previous soul lives to be brought to consciousness even from before the Fall, when human beings and earth were still fluidic and wholly united with the Godhead. The disciple learnt that the I AM, the Christ Spirit, was to be born, and felt the need to change his ways, yield up his lower ego, and return to a state of grace from which he had fallen — what Mark called (1:4) repentance for the forgiveness of sins.

Initiation had always been conducted in strictest secrecy. Now here was the Baptist doing something similar in the open (Mark 1:5). No wonder that priests were sent to find out who he was — nor that despite acceptance by them (5:35) he would soon be beheaded (Mark 6:27). But he could only save people from the consequences of the Fall by withdrawing them from the world in a baptism of remembrance. Christ however wanted people to remain in the world and yet be saved; his Baptism in the Holy

Spirit (v. 33) is one of prophecy, pointing to the future (chapters 14–16).

To touch the shoes was the menial task of a slave, forbidden to disciples. But an old sign of the zodiac for Waterman was a man stooping with arms in such a position.

1:29–34 The Baptist's Testimony — Spirit Descends and Remains

29 Next day he catches sight of Jesus coming towards him and says, Look, the Lamb of God lifting off the sin of the world. **30** This is he of whom 'I' said, After me comes one who has become prior to me, for he was before me. **31** I did not know him, but 'I' came baptizing in water so that he might be revealed to Israel. **32** And John bore witness: I have beheld the Spirit coming down as a dove out of heaven, and he remained on him. **33** I did not know him, but the one who sent me to baptize in water said to me: On whoever you perceive the Spirit descending and remaining on him, this is the one baptizing in Holy Spirit. **34** And I have seen, and have borne witness that this is the chosen one of God.

'Lamb of God' meant that Christ had descended from beyond the zodiac through the constellation of the Ram, which also formed his highest member. He brought the forces from Ram to Scales as forces for good (6:9). In the age of the Ram, Abraham had sacrificed the last clairvoyant capacity, the two-petalled lotus flower in the brow symbolized by the two horns of the ram. Now the Baptist sees the etheric body of Jesus wholly surrendered to the spirit shining through outer phenomena.

The Baptist did of course know Jesus intimately since childhood (and long before in spirit), and they had studied together with the Essenes — but he did not know that Jesus was to become the Messiah. Then he saw the Holy Spirit descend to inseminate as father (Luke 1:35) the vacated soul of Jesus. 'Thus we may compare Christ's Baptism with our begetting, his three years with our time in the womb, and his death and commitment to earth with our birth into earthly life' (3.10.13). The marginal reference to Luke (3:22) 'this day have I begotten him' is correct according to the Akashic Record (cf. Acts 13:33, Heb. 1:5, 5:5, Ps. 2:7). Thereby Jesus of Nazareth became Jesus Christ. It is correct to call 6 January (Epiphany) the day of birth of Jesus Christ.

When on earth the sun had separated, Christ (among the 'lower', stronger Gods) chose to go with the 'upper' (luciferic) gods to the sun; 'but he took with him a body of air, which enabled him now to grasp first the earthly air element, like a bird alighting—hence the evangelists likened the descent to that of a dove' (26.8.11). The dove* is an inspired imagination for the pure extract of the Eagle or Cherub element flowing from the Old Sun as radiant, shining Being. The ultimate decision to let him come was taken on the sun, the general meeting point of the Hierarchies, who gave him the forces necessary for his task. This was a deed of the Father, and was even more important than that humanity could receive him. At the same moment the power of resurrection was given.

Christ left his Spirit Man on the sun and his Life Spirit—his own lowest member—around the earth. But he brought to earth the macrocosmic ego, so that the human ego might take up this element and progress. Having been a fire spirit on Ancient Sun he streamed in at the Baptism with fire and strength, to unite with the etheric stream arising in Jesus from heart to head. 'He did not "incarnate", but "pervaded" Jesus uniquely as spiritual substance in his physical body' (14.5.12). He made use of specifically human forces alone, so that he can be understood with ordinary human understanding; but he is also there for those who seek deepest wisdom. He is the common source of all the sparks of spirit for human beings, the spirit of community. So Jesus Christ is both a cosmic and an earthly being, but with no human ego.

*For the dove as bodily archetype see T. Weihs, *Embryogenesis in Myth and Science*, Edinburgh 1986.

Christ Permeates Jesus

The Gospel next records the descent of Christ as Cosmic Ego into the astral, etheric and physical sheaths of Jesus. This involves an encounter with Lucifer and Ahriman in the sheaths, despite the purity of Jesus (of course Christ had no such karma). John is usually said not to refer to the Temptation (Matt. 4:1, Luke 4:1), but we shall find hints in the sequence tentatively described by Steiner from his research in the Akashic Record. 'This was the only time that Christ had to look into the spiritual world' (10.6.12).

Primal origin towards God (1:2).

1:35–42 First Disciples Identified — Ego-consciousness

35 Next day again, John stood with two of his disciples, 36 and gazing at Jesus as he walked, he says, Look, the Lamb of God. 37 The two disciples heard him speak, and followed Jesus. 38 Jesus turned, and observing them following, says, What do you seek? They said, Rabbi (meaning Teacher), where are you staying? 39 He says, Come and you will see. So they went and saw where he stayed, and stayed with him that day — it was about 4 p.m. 40 One of the two hearing from John and following him was Andrew, the brother of Simon Peter. 41 He first finds his own brother Simon and tells him, We have found the Messiah (which translates as Christ). 42 He led him towards Jesus, who gazed at him and said, You are Simon son of John; you shall be called Kephas (which means Peter).

This is day three of a short sequence (v. 29). Time is often mentioned because the spirit of the whole cosmos found expression in the horoscope just then. Transition from the old mysteries to the new is marked by a change of emphasis from space to time. But the starting point for ordinary ego-consciousness is 'come and see', everyday sense experience. In the last 22 verses of this chapter, five different verbs for seeing or looking occur 22 times.

'Christ' derives from *Chrestos* (Gk), the cosmic soul or sun hero (sixth degree), who 'runs with the sun'. 'He actually uses consciousness of the seventh degree (Father) which encompasses the whole of humanity' (2.11.06). 'Messiah' (Heb.) meant the anointed one.

In Matt. 16:17 Jesus calls Peter 'son of Jona(h)', so here, calling him 'son of *Ioannon*' (John) may refer to his being a pupil of the Baptist (as well as of the Essenes). Jesus grasped his essential nature — one of the best ways to perceive character is to scrutinize the walk — by calling him Kephas, Peter, the rock. This relates him to the earth element and the firm foundation of the church, as well as forecasting his loyalty. This first 'mission' is within the family.

1:43–51 The True Israelite — Astral Experience

43 Next day he wanted to go into Galilee, and finds Philip. Jesus says to him, Follow me. **44** Philip was from Bethsaida, the town of Andrew and Peter. **45** Philip finds Nathanael and tells him, We have found him of whom Moses wrote in the law, and the prophets: Jesus son of Joseph from Nazareth. **46** Nathanael: Can anything out of Nazareth be good? Philip: Come and look. **47** Jesus saw Nathanael coming towards him, and says about him, Look, truly an Israelite in whom is no deceit. **48** Nathanael: How do you Know me? Jesus: Before Philip called you, I saw you to be under the fig tree. **49** Nathanael: Rabbi, you are the son of God, you are King of Israel. **50** Jesus: Because I told you that I saw you under the fig tree, do you believe? You shall see greater things than these. **51** Truly I tell[s] you, you shall see heaven opened, and the Angels of God ascending and descending on the son of man.

This mission (day four) is among friends. Nathanael, a disciple from Cana (21:2) is traditionally identified with Bartholemew

(= son of Ptolemy), one of the Twelve. He probably knew a tradition that the Messiah would be born in Bethlehem, and Philip could not know that actually he was (Luke 2:4).

A 'true Israelite' is an initiate of the fifth degree, who has stripped off his personality and taken the folk soul into his own being, working in the realm of the Archangel. He can feel all the sorrows of his people as his own, and perform deeds of a magical kind, such as controlling the female forces in the blood. So he is an authoritative figure. Deceit is the principal vice of the consciousness soul. Bethsaida means 'house of fish'.

To be 'under the fig tree' (Bodhi tree, *arbor vitae*, tree of life) is an Egypto-Chaldean initiation symbol for deep meditation. The finely branched white tree is an imagination of the cerebellum with its related nervous system branching downwards. It gave astral insight into inner — even bodily inner — things. But this is the old, obsolete path; a new tree must spring from the wood of the cross. The verb for 'know' used here has deeper meaning than in vv. 31,33, and is henceforth capitalized.

'In occult language, the part of the human being that remains in bed was called "man", and that part born out of it in the course of evolution, namely the ego and astral body, was called the "son of man"' (25.5.08). The 'son of man' evolves upwards from below. 'When a human being evolves to the spiritual soul (consciousness soul), which very few had then done, he becomes able to receive from above the upper triad, like a blossom — the "son of God"' (11.9.10). Nathanael would not think in terms of the Trinity.

The words 'You are King of Israel' hint at the first temptation by Lucifer (acknowledge me and all shall be yours), but Christ had already defeated Lucifer on the Old Moon. The oft-to-be-repeated phrase 'Truly, truly I tell you' means, listen to your own inner being, your ego, and become aware through your own inner power of something new. 'Truly' (*amen*) is the name of the Logos himself (Rev. 3:14) but the verb is plural, it applies to everyone. So the phrase will be translated 'Truly I tell[s] you'. 'Angels of God' refer here to forces from the constellations (p. 46) that formed 'Jacob's ladder' (Gen. 28:12).

2:1–11 Marriage at Cana (First Sign) — *Etheric Working*

1 On the third day there was a marriage at Cana in Galilee. The mother of Jesus was there, **2** and Jesus and his disciples were invited to the wedding. **3** When the wine ran dry, the mother of Jesus says to him, They have no wine. **4** Jesus says to her, What to me and to you, woman. My time is not yet come. **5** His mother says to the servants, Do whatever he tells you. **6** Now lying there were six stone water jars for Jewish purification rites, each of 20–30 gallons. **7** Jesus tells them, Fill these with water. And they filled them to the brim. **8** And he tells them, Draw now, and take to the toastmaster. They did so; **9** and when he tasted the water become wine, not knowing its origin as did the servants who drew the water, he calls the bridegroom **10** and says, Every man serves first the good wine, and when they become drunk, the worse; but you have kept the good wine until now. **11** This, a beginning of the signs, Jesus did at Cana in Galilee, and manifested his splendour; and his disciples believed him inly.

This section is mainly a great prophecy of the marriage of humanity with the spirit at the transition to the coming sixth age. The 'third day' breaks the previous sequence and points to initiation (p. 77). The Galileans were of mixed blood (2 Kgs. 17:24), making it easier for Jesus Christ to work on the maternal forces.

'Alcohol has the effect of kindling a war that eliminates the ego's effect on the blood, severing the human being from the spirit world, and deadening both the memory and all comprehension of reincarnation' (20.3.13). So the Indians, Persians and Egyptians did not use it. But Noah drank wine (Gen. 9:21), and it was used in the Christian and Dionysian mysteries, because it was known that mankind had to pass through such darkness for 2000 years to learn to love the earth, and then to regain spiritual knowledge out of his ego in freedom. Christ recognized this as a temporary necessity, but this period is now passed. This may hint at the second temptation ('cast yourself down').

The Matthew Jesus child of the royal line of Solomon, who had to go to Egypt, must be distinguished from the Luke Jesus of the priestly Nathan line who was safe in Jerusalem. But at the age of 12 they became one through a magical act (Luke 2:46f.), and after deaths their families merged. The 'mother of Jesus' is here the Matthew foster-mother, to whom Jesus had passed his previous wisdom immediately before the Baptism.

The first part of v. 4 is obscure (question marks were not known) and should be translated 'This passes from me to you' — 'it refers to her maternal etheric forces, and the old blood ties of harmony and love between mother and son, which Christ is to renew' (2.7.09). Moreover the soul of the deceased Luke mother had descended and united with her at the Baptism, so that her virginity was reborn. Such was her wisdom that she then became known as the Virgin Sophia.

Christ had already permeated the elements in the time of Moses, and now the six vast jars of fresh water — representing three of body and three of soul — receive the Fullness of the six sun Elohim (1:16) within him, which he puts to work as they do in nature (15:1), working on the souls of the family members present. Then the close marriages within the group made it easier to draw out their etheric bodies to spread the taste. This points forward to 'his time', the age of Waterman, when a new form of brotherhood can be developed.

2:12–25 Cleansing the Temple — Physical Action

12 After this he went down to Capernaum with his mother, his brothers and his disciples, and stayed there a few days. **13** The Jewish Passover was near, and Jesus went up to Jerusalem. **14** In the temple he found people selling oxen, sheep and doves, and the money-changers sitting. **15** Making a lash out of ropes, he drove them all, both the sheep and the oxen, out of the temple; he poured out the coins of the money-changers and overturned the tables; **16** and he said to those selling doves, Take these away, do not make my Father's house a house of trade. **17** His disciples remembered a scripture, 'The zeal for thy house will consume me'. **18** The Jews retorted, What sign do you show us for doing these things? **19** Jesus replied, Destroy this shrine, and in three days I will raise it up. **20** The Jews said, This shrine was built in forty six years, and you will raise it in three days? **21** But He spoke about the shrine of his body. **22** So when he was raised from the dead, his disciples remembered that he had said this, and believed the scripture and the word Jesus spoke.

23 While he was in Jerusalem at the Passover feast, many believed his name inly, beholding his signs which he was doing. **24** But Jesus himself did not commit himself to them, because he Knew all people, **25** and because he had no need for anyone to testify concerning man; for he Knew what was in man.

The synoptics (Mark 11:15) place this incident at the end of the ministry as reason for Jesus' arrest. But accepting that the temple is the body (v. 21), John uses it as an imagination both for purification of the physical body by action and for the purification of the soul. Oxen, sheep and doves are powerful images of abdomen, breast and head — willing, feeling and thinking. The first two Christ purged; the third he called on those present to purge. But as regards money, the domain of Ahriman, he only upset the tables. Newly descended, he did not know that money would be necessary until the sixth epoch (seals-Rev. 6). This hints at the third temptation by Ahriman alone, and to the deed of Judas Iscariot (Matt. 26:14). 'In the sixth main epoch money-changing, trade and the desire for money will at last be driven out' (6.11.06).

The ability to rebuild the body in three days shows that Christ has already penetrated Jesus' physical body right to the bones, as no human being had ever done. As the one macrocosmic fire spirit of Ancient Sun he had unique power over the physical and chemical forces by means of a force opposed to fire which mankind does not have. He had previously given all 'things' their form (p. 13). This stupendous power, mastery over death, also enabled him to create the Resurrection Body (p. 137), with new forces for the future of evolution.

The shrine (*naon*) was the core of the temple (*ieron*) occupied by the God, as the physical body is the core of the human being created by the Hierarchies. The whole temple is purified for the

Holy Spirit, as the whole body for the spirit. Rebuilding of the temple began in 20 BC; 46 years leads to AD 26. If Jesus was 30 at the Baptism (Luke 3:23) he must have been born in 4 BC. This accords with Herod's death in 4 BC after the Matthew birth but before the Luke birth, but (p. 128) not with his death in AD 33 after three years. Perhaps the *naon* was started later than the *ieron*. The scripture (v. 17) is from Ps. 69:9.

'As a cosmic Being, Christ still comprises a great aura, which is only gradually compressed in the course of the three years to coincide with the physical body of Jesus' (3.10.13). He could at first only use the abilities already present in that body, but worked and spoke with the impressiveness of a God. His power in that body (not in himself) develops apace. Although he permeates the earth's physical substances he does not unite with them; they will be cut off.

Birth from Above

The first teaching of Christ — and the last of the Baptist — is to relate rightly to both lower and higher worlds as an equally valid experience of the highest principle: and to recognize that in Jesus are alive the occult powers of the world's origin, the world Father. The Evangelist now writes for those who know that they are out of the body and can comprehend occult truths.

All came to be through him (1.3).

3:1-12 Nicodemus — Water and Air

1 There was a man of the Pharisees named Nicodemus, a ruler of the Jews. 2 He came to Jesus by night and said, Rabbi, we know that you are a Teacher come from God, for no one can do these signs which you are doing unless God is with him. 3 Jesus: Truly I tell[s] you, unless anyone is born from above, he cannot see the kingdom of God 4 Nicodemus: how can a man be born when he is old? Can he enter a second time into his mother's womb, and be born? 5 Jesus: Truly I tell you, unless anyone is born from water and air, he cannot enter the kingdom of God; 6 that born of flesh is flesh, that born of spirit is spirit. 7 Marvel not because I told you that you must be born from above. 8 The air blows where it wishes, and you hear its sound but do not know whence it comes or whither it goes. So is everyone who is born of the spirit. 9 Nicodemus: How can these things be? 10 Jesus: Are you the teacher of Israel, and do not Know this? 11 Truly I tell you, we speak of what we know, and witness what we have seen, and none of you receive our testimony. 12 If you do not believe the earthly things I told you, how will you believe if I tell you of heavenly things?

Nicodemus, though a ruler of the Pharisees (7:50) and later a disciple (19:39) has no idea of 'birth from above', because

Judaism regarded Jehovah as an earth god – he made man from dust of earth, gave his laws in tablets of stone, appeared in a burning bush, enabled Moses to draw water from rock. Stars and their movements, lightning or thunder, worshipped by others, it regarded as influenced by Lucifer, the serpent. 'Whereas human soul life was seen to come from time, from heredity, Christ came from outside, from space, eternity, bringing brotherhood, the love of soul for soul living side by side' (27.8.09). He could move about freely in the astral world outside the body of Jesus. Still today people do not want to know about a spirit descending from above, but only believe in a highly developed human being.

That Nicodemus 'came by night' is mystery language for meeting Christ in the astral world, outside his body, through his spiritual senses. Jesus speaks of an event in the ancient mystery centres through which the pupil at about the age of 30 felt himself a completely different person – hence it was called a second birth. In contrast to natural birth through moon forces, this was regarded as a sun-birth, permeated by the Christ forces. But since Daniel and Enoch, the Jews had no initiates, only prophets reincarnated from initiates in other mysteries. So Nicodemus experienced Jehovah in the bloodstream of his people, and he would not see the need to free the higher self from the body and lower ego.

'Water and air' point to the mists before the Fall, experienced in John's baptism. (*pneuma* usually translates as 'spirit', but not here in view of vv. 8,12). 'When human beings began to breathe air, the ego could enter the oxygen' (3.11.05). The correlate is 'with fire and spirit' (Matt. 3:11) or 'in spirit and truth' (4:24).

To see the Kingdom of God means to have awoken the core of one's being, the higher ego, in one's spiritual soul. But Christ speaks of 'entering' the kingdom, which looks forward to living as Spirit Self in spiritland at the end of the seventh age, free of the body (p. 110). The essential fact here is the retention of full ego-consciousness on entering the spiritual world. But Judaism no longer had such a training. 'You' (v. 7) is plural; it can apply to every ego.

3:13-21 *God So Loved the World — Son of Man, Son of God*

13 No one has ascended into heaven except the one who has come down out of heaven, the son of man. **14** As Moses lifted up the serpent in the desert, so must the son of man be lifted up, **15** that everyone believing may have eternal life in him. **16** For God so loved the world that he gave the one-begotten son, that everyone believing him inly may not perish but may have eternal life. **17** For God sent the son into the world, not to judge the world, but that the world might be saved through him. **18** One who believes him inly is not judged; one not believing has already been judged, because he has not believed inly the name of the one-begotten son of God. **19** And this is the judgement, that the light has come into the world, and men loved the darkness rather than the light, for their deeds were evil. **20** For everyone who does evil hates the light, and does not come towards the light, lest his deeds be exposed; **21** but one doing the truth comes to the light, that it may be manifest that his deeds have been wrought in God.

Jesus is still speaking to Nicodemus, for whom 'God' was not the Father but Jehovah, one of many holy spirits. But Jehovah reflected from the sun that part of the Elohim which formed a vehicle for Christ (1:16). 'So he really resembled Christ completely, but seen in the mirror of the moon' (25.8.11). His name, YHWH, translated as 'the LORD God', really meant 'he is'.

A pupil who had become a 'son of man' in his consciousness soul no longer felt part of a family or tribe, but loved all humanity. There were already a few, such as Jeremiah, Ezekiel, the Baptist, and leaders of technology (such as Hiram), of the arts and of morality. These 'serpents' lifted up by Moses (Num. 21:9) could still become witnesses of the spiritual world above the earth through luciferic clairvoyance. They saw how luciferic beings, who had left with the sun but had to fall back, entered the human body prematurely from within, and became man's seducers, creating pride, ambition and vanity, but also human freedom and enthusiasm for the spirit.

'But the forces of the 'son of man' also bring about our destruction. It is the forces which during the first three years of childhood form us and elaborate the brain unconsciously under guidance from the Hierarchies that include all the vitalizing, health-giving forces. These are called the 'son of God', and must now be awoken consciously' (25.2.11). Through Christ the necessary forces have already been put into our astral body that can lift every 'son of man' to receive the Spirit Self; and in the sixth age the one-begotten 'son of man' must receive this spiritual power of the 'I am' from above, thus becoming a 'son of God'. For this, truth must be 'done' (v. 21).

3:22–30 The Baptist Withdraws — Christ Must Increase

22 After this, Jesus and his disciples came into Judea, and he remained there with them and baptized. **23** John was also baptizing in Aenon near Salim, because many waters were there, and they came and were baptized; **24** for John had not yet been cast into prison. **25** So John's disciples were in discussion [with a Jew] about purifying. **26** They came towards John and said, Rabbi, look, this person who was with you beyond Jordan, and to whom you bore witness, is baptizing; and they are all coming towards him. **27** John answered; A man cannot receive anything unless it has been given to him out of heaven. **28** You are my witness that I said, 'I' am not the Christ, but I am sent before Him. **29** The one who has the bride is a bridegroom; but his friend, standing and hearing him, rejoices at his voice. Therefore my joy has been fulfilled. **30** It behoves Him to increase, but me to decrease.

'Purifying' (*katharismos*) means refreshing the astral body by meditation. Jews sought union with the Divine through the group soul, but the Baptist taught the need to discover in the 'I am' the god within oneself. He sees mankind as the bride and Christ as the groom who carries consciousness of the whole of mankind in extract within him, and who brings back the part of the soul that was withheld at the Fall (Gen. 3:22), replacing hereditary bonds.

The Baptist's spiritual stature will not decrease, only his physical effects. He sees Christ as the spiritual Sun Being, whose light will increasingly shine forth from the darkness of the ordinary ego, with he himself as the sun after midsummer. Hence St John's Day is at midsummer. The old covenant of obedience to God's commands must decrease, whilst the new covenant, the love of goodness out of one's own free will, must increase.

For the Baptist, the ultimate bridegroom is Christ, who unites (marries) the evolving soul itself; but first that must ripen.

3:31–4:4 The Baptist's Valediction—All in His Hand

31 The one coming from above is over all; the one who is of the earth is of the earth and speaks of the earth. The one coming out of heaven [is over all; **32** he] testifies to what he has seen and heard, and no one receives his testimony. **33** The one who does receive his testimony authenticated that God is true. **34** For he whom God sent speaks the words of God; not in metre does he give the spirit. **35** The Father loves the Son, and has given all in his hand. **36** He who believes the Son inly has eternal life; but one disobeying the Son will not see life, but the wrath of God remains on him.

4 1 So when [the Lord knew that] the Pharisees had heard that Jesus was making and baptizing more disciples than John **2** [although Jesus himself did not baptize, but his disciples] **3** he left Judea for Galilee, **4** and had to pass through Samaria.

The Baptist was the last person able to develop higher faculties on the basis of heredity (Matt. 11:11). Now he can say that not only has Christ come 'out of heaven', so is the higher self which he brought unified with the spiritual foundations of the world. But one who comes from above speaks in such a way that the ego of the ordinary person does not receive it—otherwise he would no longer be free and independent. Everyone must sooner or later find within himself his eternal self, the lord of the soul whom the Baptist proclaimed (1:23).

He who does receive Christ's word knows that the god within him – 'I am the I am' – is true. But to say this honestly is the result of a soul struggle, not a question of saying it beautifully like the psalmist. He bears witness of God's language, even in stammering words.

The Baptist has been speaking of the One God beyond the Threshold. But after Christ has descended this side of the Threshold he finally distinguishes the Father and the Son. His statement that 'the Father has given all in his hand' is the crucial turning point of evolution (5:17,13:3, Matt. 28:18). And the deed is done. He brought the Fullness (1:16) with him for humans to grasp – the sevenfold 'I am'. 'But the time-honoured gods, or God, the Spirits of Form (Elohim) are today being replaced by the Spirits of Personality (Archai), who do not give imaginations but require human beings to make an effort to form them' (28.12.18). 'Already in the 1840s Jehovah ceased in a sense to master the opposing spirits, so that for the first time it was necessary that the Christ-impulse should be really understood' (7.12.18). The gods too continually evolve. So far as one who 'believes inly' (p. 2) has the ability to purify and transform the etheric body – temperament, inclinations and habits – so far has he the Son, the Logos, within him. All levels of the spiritual world must be regarded as being in progressive (or retrogressive) metamorphosis.

Awakening the 'I'

This chapter speaks in symbolic form of the influx of the Christ principle into human nature at large, awakening the 'I'.

Without him nothing came to be (1:3).

4:5–15 The Woman of Samaria — Living Water

5 He comes into a town of Samaria called Sychar, near the plot which Jacob gave to his son Joseph; **6** and Jacob's spring was there. So Jesus, wearied by his journey, sat thus about midday at the spring. **7** A woman of Samaria comes to draw water, and Jesus says to her, Give me a drink; **8** for his disciples had gone into the town to buy food. **9** Woman: How is it that you, a Jew, ask a drink from me, a Samaritan woman? [For Jews do not associate with Samaritans.] **10** Jesus: If you knew the bounty of God, and who says to you, give me a drink, you would have asked him, and he would have given you living water. **11** Woman: Sir, you have no pail, and the well is deep; whence do you get the living water? **12** Are you greater than our father Jacob, who gave us the well, and himself drank from it, and his sons and his cattle? **13** Jesus: Everyone drinking this water will thirst again; **14** but whoever has drunk of the water that 'I' will give him will never thirst again, but the water that I will give him will become in him a spring of water welling up into eternal life. **15** Woman: Sir, give me this water, that I neither thirst nor come hither to draw.

That Jesus went to Samaria, a people of the most mixed blood (p. 25), indicates that his mission was for all individual souls. Think back to Jacob, who *c.* 1900 BC fathered the twelve tribes of Israel. Contrast Joseph, who flourished in Egypt using the old clairvoyance, with his brothers, who were the first to receive revelations from the sense-world and rational thinking. It is noteworthy that Jesus is alone, without his disciples, when he meets this lone woman, awakens her memory (*etheric body*), and speaks the word 'I' for the first time (v. 13).

The living water Jesus mentions here is not just fresh running water (as 2:7), but the first hint in symbolic form of the influx of the Christ principle into human nature. At Cana he had transformed the water; now he shows that he lives in the elements. Through his force the etheric bodies of those who find access to him become radiant with an impulse that exhales life and is immortal. 'We are spiritually in a desert until we find this water, which will well up out of the "I" from spiritland. It is a new source of knowledge of good and evil, replacing the law of Moses' (30.10.06). Christianity contains the secret of how man can gradually develop himself towards resurrection of the etheric body. Christ promises the new Waterman forces to come.

4:16–26 The New Worship — 'I' Am

16 Jesus: Go, call your husband and come here. **17** Woman: I have no husband. Jesus: You say well, I have no husband; **18** you had five husbands, and he whom you now have is not your husband; this you spoke truly. **19** Woman: Sir, I perceive that you are a prophet. **20** Our fathers worshipped on this mountain, and you say that in Jerusalem is where one should worship. **21** Jesus: Believe me, woman, a time is coming when neither on this mountain nor in Jerusalem will you worship the Father. **22** You worship what you do not know; we worship what we know [because salvation is from the Jews]. **23** But a time comes, and now is, when true worshippers will worship the Father in spirit and truth; for indeed the Father seeks such to worship him. **24** God is [a] spirit, and those worshipping must worship in spirit and truth. **25** Woman: I know that Messiah, called Christ, is coming; when he comes, he will expound everything to us. **26** Jesus: 'I' am, the one speaking to you.

'The five husbands here contrast the five non-physical principles on which past worship could have been based — physical, etheric and astral (sentient) bodies, and the sentient and rational souls—with the new principle of the 'I', which is free, i.e. "has not a husband"' (21.11.07). She was to be raised to the higher self, her 'new husband'.

Judaism required worship in one place only (Deut. 12:14). Abraham, Jacob (and the Samaritans said Moses) had built altars on Mount Gerizim. The Samaritan temple had been destroyed, and the destruction of that in Jerusalem was immanent. The Samaritans had only the first five books of the Bible, so her knowledge of the Messiah suggests special insight.

Worship in spirit and truth (v. 24) means knowledge in clarity of higher consciousness of that which is beyond the threshold, not mere belief. Today it can only be safely reached through anthroposophy.

Eimi means: I am. So *ego eimi* will be translated: 'I' am or 'I am'. But each of us can say it of our higher self.

4:27-42 My Food is to Do His Will—We Ourselves Have Heard

27At this his disciples came back, and were surprised that he was speaking with a woman; but no one asked, What do you want, or, Why do you speak with her? **28** So she left her water jar and went into the town, and says to the men: **29** Come, see a man who told me all that I did—could this be the Christ? **30** They left the town and came towards him.

31 Meanwhile the disciples invited him, Rabbi, eat. **32** But he said, 'I' have food to eat of which you do not know. **33** The disciples said to one another, Has anyone brought him food? **34** Jesus: My food is that I may do the will of the one who sent me, and may complete his work. **35** Do you not say, It is yet four months until harvest? I tell you, lift up your eyes, and behold the fields white to harvest. **36** Already the reaper receives wages, and gathers fruit into eternal life, that sower and reaper may rejoice together. **37** For in this the saying is true, that one sows and another reaps. **38** 'I' sent you to reap that on which you have not worked; others have worked, and you have entered into their work.

39 Many Samaritans of that town had believed him inly because of the woman's witness: He told me all that I did. **40** So when they reached him they asked him to stay with them; and he stayed there a couple of days. **41** And many more believed because of his word; **42** and they said to the woman, We no longer believe because of your talk; for we have heard for ourselves, and we know that this is truly the Saviour of the world.

The woman springs into action (*sentient body*) and undertakes the fifth mission, now extended to a town.

This next interpolation relates the 'I' to the physical bodily processes. With every sense perception we receive a threefold spiritual impulse which nourishes the body. 'We only need earthly substance from the metabolism for our head, to enable it to support our ego; the drink suffices him. The rest of our body derives from cosmic substance drawn from "the light, air and warmth forces of the Sun-Elohim, which Jesus has within him" (1:16) (16.6.24). He had already gone 40 days without food at the Temptation' (Luke 4:2).[*]

The higher 'I' receives the wages of a previous life and gathers fruit for future lives—it is both sower and reaper. Moreover future involution is a transmutation of evolution hitherto; our fifth age is a transformation of the third (Amos 9:13).

Though the first disciples stayed with Jesus (1:39), he now stays with the Samaritans, which may again imply teaching 'by night' (3:2). Conviction because they 'heard for themselves' is characteristic of the *sentient soul*. The female element makes development possible, then Christ enables the male element to receive the spirit.

4:43–54 The Official's Son (Second Sign) — The Value of Belief

43 After the two days he went on into Galilee. **44** For Jesus himself testified that a prophet has no honour in his own

---

[*]See *Life from Light*, M. Werner & T. Stockli, Clairview 2007.

country. **45** When he came into Galilee the Galileans welcomed
him, having seen all that he did in Jerusalem at the festival, for
they too went to it. **46** So he came again to Cana of Galilee where
he made the water into wine. And there was a certain royal
official whose son was ill in Capernaum. **47** Hearing that Jesus
had come from Judea into Galilee, this person went to him and
asked him to come down and cure his son, for he was about to
die. **48** Jesus: Unless you people see signs and wonders you do
not believe. **49** The official: Sir, come down before my child dies.
50 Jesus: Go, your son lives. The man believed the word Jesus
said to him, and went. **51** While he was going down the bond-
servants met him, saying that his boy lives. **52** He asked them
what time he got better, so they said, Yesterday about 1 p.m. the
fever left him. **53** The father knew that this was the time when
Jesus said, Your son lives. And he and his whole household
believed. **54** This was a second sign that Jesus did, having come
out of Judea into Galilee.

The official whose boy is near death represents the Roman age,
dying from lack of knowledge of the spirit. In that age healing as
such was not uncommon; physicians could, through feeling,
channel forces from supersensible worlds, and heal by the effect
of the word.

'Jesus could now kindle the forces of the father's *intellectual
soul*, namely belief, and work in unison with him on the boy even
at a distance. Had the father not believed, the boy could not have
recovered' (2.7.09). Faith based on knowledge is the most
important force of the astral body. Christ still lived in his whole
environment to such an extent that he could pass over from one
person to another, and again works ignoring politics and class.

The New Will

For 29 verses Jesus speaks as the Son, only once as 'I'. The higher self of the Evangelist stood clearly before his inner eye, and he knew: This is 'I'; it will gradually descend on me as it did on him whom I followed. In the distant future this divine man will arise resurrected in every human being.

What has become in him was Life (1:4).

5:1–16 Healing at the Pool (Third Sign) — Get Up and Walk

1 After this there was a feast of the Jews, and Jesus went up to Jerusalem. **2** In Jerusalem there is at the sheep [gate] a pool in Hebrew called Bethesda, which has five colonnades. **3** In these lay a multitude of invalids, blind, lame, withered, [waiting for the moving of the water; **4** for an Angel of the Lord went down at certain times into the pool and disturbed the water; whoever stepped in first after the disturbing of the water was healed of whatever disease he had]. **5** One man there had been ill for 38 years. **6** Seeing him lying there and Knowing he has already been there a long time, Jesus says, Have you the will to become whole? **7** The invalid said, Sir, I have no man to put me into the pool when the water is disturbed, but while 'I' am coming, another goes down before me. **8** Jesus says, Get up, take your pallet and walk. **9** Immediately the man became whole, and took his pallet and walked. That day was a sabbath. **10** So the Jews said to the one who was healed, It is a sabbath, and it is not lawful for you to take the pallet. **11** But he answered, The one who made me whole, he told me, Take your pallet and walk. **12** They asked him, Who is the man telling you to take it and walk? **13** But the one healed did not know who it was, for Jesus withdrew because there was a crowd there. **14** Later Jesus finds him in the temple and said, See, you are healed; sin no more, lest something worse happens to you. **15** The man went away and told the Jews that it was Jesus who had healed him. **16** Consequently the Jews [began to] persecute Jesus for doing this on a sabbath.

Sheep for sacrifice were washed in the pool of Bethesda (house of two springs). 'Its special powers were reputedly due to having had dropped into it a piece of wood from the burning bush (Exod. 3:2) bearing the words "I am the I am" (and from which the cross would be made) – an image of new life from that which is dying' (15.12.06). As it is not known today that Angels incarnate in moving water v. 4 is often omitted.

After 19 years sun, moon and earth are in the same relationship: thinking, feeing and willing have gone through all possibilities. So 38 years represents two incarnations between Golgotha and Christ's appearing in the etheric, during which the 'I' is acquired by the *consciousness soul*. This leads to the present age, unable to receive angelic help.

Sin is the fault of the astral body, and can cause severe illness in the next incarnation (p. 66). Since the man can freely say 'I' (v. 4), Jesus knows that the karma of his sin is fulfilled. The point is his challenge to the will, which the law (thou shalt not) does not do.

This is the first true activation of the Christ-impulse, the manifestation of the first of the six Elohim which he brought with him. Healing is thus the special impulse of Christ in our age. When the sun is in the right position, the life-endowing sun force of Christ surges through Jesus so strongly that the etheric body becomes freer to heal the physical. He penetrates directly to the man's moral depths – another extension of his power in Jesus. He thus heals through the individual spirit – the etheric body can be inwardly changed.

But to the Jews the important factor was not the healing but the sabbath. If however the sabbath is truly sanctified, souls will be specially strengthened.

5:17–30 From Father to Son – Spiritual Evolution

17 But he answered, My Father works until now, and 'I' work. **18** For this the Jews sought the more to kill him, because he not only violated the sabbath but also said that God was his own father, making himself equal to God. **19** Jesus responded: Truly I tell[s] you, the Son cannot do anything from himself except what he sees the Father doing; for whatever He does, the Son does likewise. **20** For the Father is devoted to the Son, and shows him all that he does; and he will show him greater deeds than these, that you may be full of wonder. **21** For as the Father raises and brings to life the dead, so the Son brings to life whom he will. **22** For the Father judges no one, but has given all judgment to the Son, **23** that everyone may honour the Son as they do the Father. One who does not honour the Son does not honour the Father who sent him. **24** Truly I tell[s] you, one who hears my word and believes him who sent me has eternal life, and does not come into judgment, but has passed over out of death into life.

25 Truly I tell[s] you, a time comes and now is, when the dead will hear the voice of the Son [of God], and those who listen will live. **26** For as the Father has life in himself, so he gave to the Son to have life in himself. **27** And he gave him authority to effect judgment, because he is [a] son of man. **28** Do not be astonished at this, because a time comes when all those in tombs will hear his voice, **29** and come forth, those who have done good to resurrection of life, those who have done evil to resurrection of judgment. **30** 'I' cannot do anything from myself; as I hear, I judge; and my judgment is just, because I seek not my own will, but the will of him who sent me.

Behind the whole galaxy stands the Father, who also manifests in our actions. He is the world-creative universal Will, the most evolved Spirit of Ancient Saturn (though where Saturn and Sun were unknown the Moon was regarded as Father). Outer things perceptible everywhere around us, including physical, etheric and astral bodies in nature, and death itself, are in truth rooted in the Father, though distorted for us by Lucifer and Ahriman. But 'heaven and earth shall pass away' (Matt. 24:35).

Christ is directly connected with Ancient Sun evolution, when he evolved the macrocosmic ego outside earthly conditions. He is now to be found by following the path of the soul as a historical being. (All eastern cultures treated time like the seasons. Only the Old Testament had a concept of history.) He brings new life, redemption, involution which 'will not pass away' to the Father's creation. Now that physical bodies are crumbling, he can bring the 'I' to consciousness within them.

'The astral body is partly controlled by the ego, and partly under control by our Angel, who guides the human being from one incarnation to another. When the ego is in complete control we call our higher principle *Spirit Self* (p. 48). Whether we say that we look up to our higher self or to our Angel is exactly the same in a spiritual sense' (6.8.08). This higher ego does not enter the body, but has eternal life (v. 24). Thus the 'I am' can experience itself as instrument of the Cosmic Ego, Saturn or Sun.

Raising the dead to life was always the task of the mysteries (e.g. 1 Kgs. 17:22), and Christ has power over death because he is master (2:19) of the forces of the physical body. Since he 'knew what is in man' (2:25) he could judge (assess) the extent of 'the sins of the world', and the consequent deterioration of the original archetype or phantom since the Fall. But his judgement differs from ours in being totally objective. See p. 60.

The past tense in vv. 22,26,27 confirms that the transition has taken place from the Father's law to Christian action out of love in freedom, as 3:35 and 13:3 emphasize. The usual translation 'God continues to work' is an inaccurate interpretation (p. 34).

5:31-47 *The Baptist is Dead—Scripture or My Deeds*

31 If 'I' testify about myself, my testimony is not true. **32** There is another who bears witness concerning me, and I know that the testimony that he affirms about me is true. **33** You sent to John, and he witnessed to the truth; **34** but 'I' receive witness not from [a] man—I say these things that you may be saved. **35** He was the burning and shining lamp, and you were willing for a while to rejoice in his light. **36** But 'I' have witness greater than that of John; for the tasks that the Father has given me to complete, the very deeds I do, bear me witness that the Father has sent me. **37** And the Father who sent me, He has borne witness concerning me. You have never heard his voice nor seen his form, **38** and you do not have his word abiding in you, because you do not believe him whom He has sent. **39** You pore over the scriptures, because you think to have in them eternal life, and they testify concerning me; **40** yet you do not wish to come to me that you may have life. **41** I do not receive honour from men, **42** but I Know that you do not have the love of God within you. **43** 'I' have come in the name of my Father, and you do not accept me; yet if another comes in his own name you will accept him. **44** How can you believe, who accept honour from one another, yet do not seek honour from the only God? **45** Do not think that 'I' will accuse you to the Father; Moses is the one accusing you, in whom you have hoped. **46** For if you believed Moses you would have believed me; for he wrote about me. **47** But if you do not believe what he wrote, how will you believe my words?

The Baptist remained widely after his death (Mark 6:34) as an 'atmosphere' among his disciples, into whom Christ worked most easily, with compassion for their loss. As bearer of the powers of Elijah he also remained in a special way among the Twelve, as a kind of group soul, and above all with the Evangelist.

In all that becomes fixed through writing or printing there is the ahrimanic element—libraries great and small are citadels of Ahriman. Even Moses misinterpreted when 'Christ himself appeared in the burning bush (Exod. 3:2) and in the fire on Sinai (Exod. 31:18)—none but he said "I am the I am"' (10.4.09). His gradual descent had been observed in the mysteries (Luke 24:27), but the Jews regarded this as being 'through' an angel (Acts 7:35), so did not recognize it.

Cosmic Nourishment

Behind the whole universe stands the Father. These forces not only nourish Jesus (4:32), but he passes them through his disciples to those seeking him.

The Life was the Light of Men. (1:4)

6:1–5 Feeding the Five Thousand (Fourth Sign) – The New Communion

1 After this Jesus went away across the Sea of Galilee (of Tiberias). 2 A large crowd followed, because they saw the signs that he did on the sick. 3 Jesus went up into the mountain and sat there with his disciples. 4 The Jewish Passover was near. 5 Raising his eyes and seeing a large crowd coming towards him, Jesus says to Philip: Where can we buy loaves for these to eat? 6 This he said to test him, for he knew what he was going to do. 7 Philip answered, £20 worth of loaves are not enough for each to take a little. 8 One of his disciples, Andrew brother of Simon Peter, says 9 There is a lad here who has five barley loaves and two fishes, but what are these among so many? 10 Jesus said, make the people sit down. There was plenty of grass, so the men sat down, numbering about five thousand. 11 Jesus took the loaves, and having given thanks, he distributed them [to the disciples, and the disciples] to those seated; also of the fishes, as much as they wanted. 12 When they were filled, he tells his disciples: gather the fragments left over, that nothing be lost. 13 So they gathered up, and filled twelve baskets with fragments of the five barley loaves left by those who had eaten. 14 Seeing what sign he did, the people said, This is truly the prophet coming into the world. 15 So Jesus, knowing that they were about to come and seize him to make him king, withdrew again alone into the mountain.

Jesus first withdraws with his disciples, as he does for the 'sermon on the mount' (Matt. 5:1). This means that he gives them esoteric instruction to rouse their consciousness when together to a new kind of clairvoyance, awakening a power in their etheric bodies which leads to spiritland beyond space and time, the first stage of initiation. A mountain is more conducive to inspiration than the plain.

Zodiac forces represent the very oldest divine-spiritual beings from Ancient Saturn, the Father forces, whom the Twelve were chosen to represent. On the Ancient Sun, Christ had received in himself the original being of these twelve World Initiators. The five 'loaves' symbolize the five 'night' constellations from Fishes to Scorpion that are now descending to humanity, and the two 'fishes' represent Ram and Scales that separate them from those ascending. These forces correspond to the physical, etheric and astral bodies, ego and Spirit Self, augmented by Life Spirit and 'the mystical lamb'. They relate specifically to the metabolic-limb system, the centre for the formation of blood as instrument of the ego (7:38), hence the men (sic) had to sit down.

'The most significant aspect is Christ's giving thanks (eucharistie), which calls down spiritual nourishment from the cosmos' (2.7.09). The transformation of bread is a clairvoyant act, passing in a flash but seen by the disciples, who beheld in far-reaching pictures the evolution of humanity from the fourth to the fifth age (p. 100). Through their forces of active goodness which had just been ripened, they could distribute the power emanating from the mighty etheric body of Christ to enliven the souls permeated by the newly deceased Elijah-John, who had increased bread before (1 Kgs. 7:14 & 2 Kgs. 4:42). This was 'as much as they wanted'; it was a spiritual not a physical meal. The 'remains' are those of Christ's etheric body, necessarily in twelve measures.

The synoptics describe also the feeding of the four 'thousand', from which only seven basketfuls remained, the ascending constellations from the past — Christ here brings those for the future.

6:16–21 Appearing on the Water (Fifth Sign) — Spirit Sight

16 When evening came his disciples went down to the sea, **17** embarked on a boat, and came across the sea to Capernaum.

Darkness had now come, and Jesus had not yet come to them. **18** As a great wind blew the sea was roused. **19** After rowing three miles or more, they behold Jesus walking on the sea and nearing the boat, and were afraid. **20** But he says to them, 'I' am, fear not. **21** So they wanted to take him into the boat, and immediately the boat was at the land to which they were going.

John does not say that Jesus walked on the sea, but that the disciples beheld this. Mark (6:48) and Matthew (14:25) add that 'they thought it was a phantom'. Water forms a threshold between earth and air, used in a Waterman initiation. 'Being on water is specially suited to the perception of Imaginations, and vision at a distance is such that the image appears in the immediate vicinity of the seer' (2.7.09). Christ enables the forces of Imagination to stream to the disciples; he comes to them astrally, not physically. 'I am' is the name used for Christ by the disciples, so it is an inner spiritual reality which stiffens their egos. The usual 'It is I' is inaccurate.

6:22–7 *Found Across the Sea — Because You Ate the Loaves*

22 Next day the crowd standing across the sea saw that there was only one small boat there, and that Jesus did not get into the boat with his disciples, but that they went away alone. **23** Other boats came from Tiberius near the place where they ate the bread, [the Lord having given thanks]. **24** So when the crowd saw that neither Jesus nor his disciples were there, they embarked onto the boats and came into Capernaum seeking Jesus. **25** And finding him across the sea they said, Rabbi, when did you come here? **26** Jesus replied, Truly I tell[s] you, you seek me not because you saw signs, but because you ate of the loaves and were satisfied. **27** Work not for perishable food, but for the food enduring to eternal life, which the son of man will give you; for on him God the Father set his seal.

While Jesus was again on the mountain (v. 15) even the crowd who sought him, now in Capernaum, 'found him across the sea' by the same means of Imagination as the disciples, the image again appearing near to them. As pupils of the Baptist they had penetrated the veil of the outer world, and 'the first stage of initiation consists of learning to "look back" from the other side' (9.10.05). The sun forces of Christ are extended, and the crowd are still within his mighty aura. They saw 'signs', but it was the cosmic forces, the 'loaves', which satisfied them. Those at a distance whose souls Christ had united with his own could behold in spirit his very form as he reflected to them the nocturnal sun forces. Thus the deeds of the disciples are multiplied. The human being continually receives soul-spiritual nourishment out of the spiritual world.

6:28–36 'I Am the Bread of Life* — Life Spirit

28 So they asked him, What should we do, to do the works of God? **29** Jesus replied, This is the work of God, that you believe inly him whom He sent. **30** So they said, What sign then do you do, that we may see, and believe you? What deed do you perform? **31** Our fathers ate manna in the desert, as it is written, Bread out of heaven he gave them to eat. **32** Jesus replied, Truly I tell[s] you, not Moses gave you the bread out of heaven, but my Father gives you the true bread out of heaven. **33** For the bread of God is the one coming down out of heaven and giving life to the world. **34** So they said to him, Lord give us always this bread. **35** Jesus said, 'I' am the bread of life; one who comes to me never hungers, one who believes me inly will never thirst. **36** But I told you that you have both seen [me] and do not believe.

At the time of Moses (who was only the instrument) the Logos, the 'I am', flowed as 'manna' (Exod. 16:35) or manas, the first trace of *Spirit Self*. It could be taken in through the senses into the blood, and understood by the intellect. As the wisdom of nature this is the lowest substance of the Elohim/Exusiai. But by uniting

---

*First stage of development of the 'I am'.

the etheric with the physical this has also since Lemuria been the cause of death.

The constellations are in themselves beyond good and evil, but they have varied effects on descending into time or ascending. They give real life to the soul and nourishment to the ego in its solitude, but cannot be understood by the intellect. They are not just teaching or concept, but are the forces of cosmic Life (life ether) withheld at the Fall. In him is Life (1:4). Since the mid-Atlantian period Christ has expressed the successive manifestations of the members of his Being through the seven constellations from Scales to Ram, which are now ascending.

Now these forces of the heavens (the 'loaves') have become the daily bread of life. Bread was first produced through the work of Cain, whose deed Christ now takes upon himself. He had first offered life to the Samaritan woman through water (4:10); now he feels himself as part of the solid earth element, as bread—he descended not for himself but for humanity. ' 'I' am the bread of life means the *Life Spirit* to be brought forth within every 'I' in so far as we represent Christ' (25.5.08). Life Spirit is the Sun Logos entombed within earthly matter, which must be resurrected. This enables the pupil to live outside the body, which is the start of his conscious expansion to the macrocosm.

6:37–50 *My Father's Will—I Will Raise Him Up*

37 All whom the Father gives to me will come towards me, and one who comes towards me I will never cast out, **38** because I have come down from heaven, not to do my will but the will of the one who sent me. **39** And this is the will of the one who sent me, that I shall not lose any of all that he has given to me, but shall raise it up in the last day. **40** For it is my Father's will that everyone beholding the Son and believing him inly may have eternal life, and 'I' will raise him up in the last day.

41 The Jews murmured about him because he said, 'I' am the bread which came down out of heaven. **42** They said, Is not this fellow Jesus son of Joseph, whose father and mother we know? How does he now say, I have come down out of heaven? **43** Jesus answered, Do not mutter with one another. **44** No one can come to me unless the Father who sent me should draw him, and 'I' will raise him up in the last day. **45** It is written in the prophets: 'And they shall all be taught by God.' Everyone who hears and learns from the Father comes to me. **46** Not that anyone has seen the Father except the one from God, this one has seen the Father. **47** Truly I tell[s] you, he who believes has eternal life. **48** 'I' am the bread of life. **49** Your fathers ate the manna in the desert and died. **50** This is the bread coming down out of heaven that anyone may eat and not die.

The Hebrews saw themselves as entirely connected with the earth, and indeed with elements coming from inside the earth. They saw Jehovah as an earth god (p. 30). Whereas nations around them looked for their religious symbols in the stars and the atmosphere, the ancient Hebrews felt that everything coming from above, from outside the earth, had to do with Lucifer, who had remained at the Moon stage of evolution. So when Jesus said that his Father had sent him down from heaven, he met strong opposition (which still exists). Unless the 'I' is filled with the cosmic forces (the loaves) it cannot be raised up (v. 44), but this is open to everyone (v. 50).

The 'last day' is preceded by the 'first death', the end of the physical body (Rev. 20:5) and the 'second death', the end of the etheric body (Rev. 20:14) and is thus seen as the ending of the astral body. Thereafter all is again spirit, as in the origin of time, but transformed by the whole evolution of Earth. The quotation referred only to 'sons of Jerusalem' (Isa. 54:13), but eternal life (p. 43) can already be gained now by anyone through belief in Christ (v. 47).

6:51–65 My Flesh and Blood — Spirit Gives Life

51 'I' am the living bread that came down out of heaven; if anyone eats of this bread he will live forever; and indeed the bread which 'I' will give is my flesh for the life of the world. **52** The Jews contended with one another, saying, How can this fellow give us [his] flesh to eat? **53** Jesus replied, Truly I tell[s] you, unless you eat the flesh of the son of man and drink his blood, you have no life in you. **54** He who eats my flesh and drinks my blood has life eternal, and I will raise him up in the last day. **55** For my flesh is true food, and my blood is true drink. **56** He who eats my flesh and drinks my blood abides in me, and I in him. **57** As the living Father sent me, and I live because of the Father, so the one eating me will also live because of me. **58** This is the bread which came down out of heaven, not such as the fathers ate, and died; he who eats this bread will live for ever. **59** This he said, teaching in a synagogue in Capernaum.

60 Many of his disciples, hearing it, said, This is a difficult word — who can listen to it? **61** But Jesus, knowing in himself that his disciples are murmuring about it, said to them, Does this hinder you? **62** What if you behold the son of man ascending to where he was at first? **63** It is [the] Spirit that gives life, the flesh is of no avail. The words 'I' have spoken to you are spirit and are life. **64** But there are some of you who do not believe. For Jesus knew from the start who did not believe, and who was the betrayer. **65** And he said, That is why I told you that no one can come towards me unless it is given to him by the Father.

As the Sun Spirit becomes the new Spirit of the Earth (p. 130), every atom of the earth, every morsel of food and drink, has become part of Christ's body — not only that which is consecrated by a priest. Such a thought in our heart attracts his body and blood in the substance of bread and juices. The vehicle to receive him as Life Spirit must be formed in the bloodstream as it rises from the heart to the head (7:38), so that 'the blood, the expression of the ego, will eventually be felt to be the appearance of the etheric Christ' (1.10.11). But the Logos, the Word, comprises forces from the fixed stars (consonants) and the solar system (vowels). Thus his 'flesh' is a cosmic force-impulse in which one who has eaten the bread (v. 13) can participate. He gives us part of his being if we so will it.

This spiritual interpretation was (necessarily) lost during the later Middle Ages, and authoritatively changed into the idea of a physical transformation. But Jews were forbidden to take blood (Lev. 17:12). Without this spiritual impulse the earth would be dead, and lead to a dead Jupiter.

At the Abyss

John here experiences separation from the body and awakening to the soul world. Thereafter, thinking, feeling and willing go their separate ways unless controlled by the 'I'. We cannot enter the spiritual world without a kind of inner shattering, which we must meet with outward equanimity.

And the Light shone in the Darkness (1:5).

6:66–7:13 The Twelve and the Brothers — Doubt, Hatred, Fear

66 From this, many of his disciples drew back and no longer went about with him. **67** So Jesus said to the Twelve, Do you not also wish to go? **68** Simon Peter answered, Lord, to whom should we go? You have words of eternal life; **69** and we have believed and Known that you are the Holy One of God. **70** Jesus replied, Did not 'I' choose you, the Twelve, and one of you is a devil? **71** He spoke of Judas son of Simon Iscariot, for he, one of the Twelve, was about to betray him.

7:1 After this Jesus went about in Galilee, for he would not go about in Judea because the Jews were seeking to kill him. **2** Now the Jewish feast of Tabernacles was near. **3** So his brothers said to him, Set off and go into Judea, that your disciples also will see your deeds that you are doing; **4** for no one does a thing in secret who seeks to be in the open himself. If you do these things, show yourself to the world. **5** For his brothers did not believe in him. **6** Jesus says to them, My time has not yet come, but your time is always at hand. **7** The world cannot hate you, but it hates me because 'I' testify that its deeds are evil. **8** You go up to the feast, for 'I' do not [yet] go up to this feast, because my time has not yet been completed. **9** And saying this to them, he remained in Galilee.

10 But when his brothers had gone up to the feast, then he also went up, not publicly but in private. **11** The Jews were looking for him at the feast and said, Where is he? **12** And there was much murmuring about him in the crowds; some said, He is good; but others said, No, he deceives the crowd. **13** No one however spoke openly about him for fear of the Jews.

The Twelve are mentioned three times, but nowhere else. In them appeared again the five sons of Mattathias (1 Macc. 2:2) and the seven Maccabean sons (2 Macc. 7:1) (John has only named five). Like the twelve knights of King Arthur or Barbarossa, as always provided by the mysteries at this point, they bear the cosmic forces (6:13) which counteract the twelve demons (Mark 7:21). Many followers of Jesus withdraw from doubts about his teaching; he is tempted to go prematurely to Jerusalem (v. 3) but declines because of the hatred he will meet (v. 7). When he does go, he finds a mood of fear (v. 13). 'Now doubt, hatred and fear are the "three beasts", the distortions of thinking, feeling and willing, that always arise from the abyss at the threshold to the spiritual world' (15.2.24). Inner impulses, desires and passions wax strong and powerful; they try to capture us, horrify us or repel us, with immeasurable arrogance. 'To develop the thought-filled ego, we all bear within us a fury of material destruction, which is the cause of unconscious fear. This must be filled by moral and ethical deeds, out of which a new nature can arise' (23/24.9.21).

Jesus has four foster-brothers and their two sisters (Mark 6:3), traditionally born after the return from Egypt. He goes to the feast as teacher, the opposite of doubt; he heals, a deed of love, not hate; and he testifies fearlessly that the deeds of the world are evil. John often writes as though the sun forces were in a body of flesh when in reality Christ is moving from place to place in spirit. His influence spreads not through understanding but through enthusiastic will. Versification (6:66) is not original, but has been ascribed to a French Calvinist printer in 1555.

7:14–24 Teaching in the Temple—Murder or Madness?

14 Then in the middle of the feast, Jesus went up into the temple and taught. **15** The Jews began to marvel, saying, How is this fellow so learned, when he has not studied? **16** Jesus replied, My teaching is not my own, but from him who sent me. **17** If anyone's will is to do his will, he will Know whether the teaching is from God, or whether 'I' speak from myself. **18** He who speaks from himself seeks his own honour, but he who seeks the honour of him who sent him is truthful, and falseness is not in him. **19** Did not Moses give you the law? Yet none of you keep the law. Why do you seek to kill me? **20** The people answered, You have a demon — who seeks to kill you? **21** Jesus replied, I did one deed, and you all marvel because of it. **22** Moses gave you circumcision (not that it is from Moses, but from the patriarchs) and you circumcise a man on a sabbath — **23** if a man receives circumcision on a sabbath so that the law of Moses is not broken, are you angry with me because I made a whole man healthy on a sabbath? **24** Do not judge superficially, but with righteous judgment.

On the basis that the temple is Christ's body (2:21), and that he has to constrict his great aura further into a human body, from here to 8:59 is the climax of his incorporation. Long before, he had taught 'as one of the Exusiai and not as the scribes' (Mark 1:22), i.e. not as Folk Spirit or Time Spirit but as one who received revelation from a power of nature, light or air, thunder or lightning.

Jesus then stands between the threat of the Jews to kill him (Ahriman) and the people's accusation of madness (Lucifer). Both Lucifer and Ahriman are met again at the Threshold, but having already confronted them he responds with righteous judgement. The 'one deed' refers to 5:1-9, the only 'sign' yet done in Jerusalem, but compare 2:23, v. 31.

Circumcision derived from Abraham, and was to be done on the eighth day after birth, even if a sabbath (Lev. 12:3, Gen. 17:12). 'A whole man' (*anthropos*) means body, soul *and* spirit (1 Thess. 5:23).

7:25-36 The Search for Christ — You Will Not Find Me

25 Some of the people of Jerusalem accordingly said, Is not this the one they seek to kill? **26** Look, he speaks openly, and they say nothing to him—might the rulers indeed know that this is the Christ? **27** Yet we know where he is from; but when the Christ comes, no one Knows where he is from. **28** So as he taught in the temple, Jesus proclaimed: You know me, and whence I am. I have not come of myself; but he who sent me, whom you do not know, is true. **29** 'I' know him because I am from him, and he sent me. **30** So they sought to arrest him, but no one laid hand on him because his time had not yet come. **31** But many of the crowd believed in him and said, when the Christ comes, will he do more signs than this one did? **32** The Pharisees heard the crowd murmuring these things about him, and the chief priests and Pharisees sent guards to arrest him. **33** So Jesus said, Yet a short time I am with you, and I go to the one who sent me. **34** You will seek me and not find me, and where I am 'I' you cannot come. **35** The Jews said to themselves, where is this fellow going, that we shall not find him? Is he about to go to the dispersion among the Greeks, to teach the Greeks? **36** What is this word that he said, You will seek me and not find me, and where I am 'I' you cannot come?

The crowd in Jerusalem is still at the stage of sign-consciousness (rational soul), they argue about the lower self of Jesus—where he comes from, where he is going, the question of his arrest. Jesus does not explain his physical origin but that of Christ. After feeling deepest pain and fullest delight we must be absolutely alone with our ideas. Then for the first time we may feel inspired by the spirit. In Inspiration the ego is silenced and the spirit manifests objectively in contrast to the dead form of the law. This is part of the search for Christ's guidance. Anyone who felt in his ego that he was 'sent from God' would understand the words of Christ without all the ancient laws and artificialities. 'True Christianity will not be a looking to Christ, but a being filled by Christ' (16.10.21).

It is not only that Christ will soon go to the Father and the tomb be empty. The real human being is invisible to physical senses; we see only the material substance that fills the bodily form. The Pharisees cannot experience the higher self because they found God only in nature, not in the soul, and hence proclaimed him through the bloodstream and unconscious will (adherence to commandments).

v. 34 is the first public hint of making known the mysteries of death and resurrection, so could not be understood. In v. 35 the words *ego eimi* (p. 37) are reversed: I am 'I'. 'That is Christ's only name, used by the most intimate initiates' (20.5.08). In every single one of us there lives a divine man who in the distant future will arise resurrected.

7:37–53 *Come to Me and Drink — Metabolic Life*

37 On the last, great day of the feast, Jesus stood up and proclaimed: If anyone thirsts, let [him] come to me and drink[.] 38 He who believes me inly, as the scripture says, Out of his belly will flow streams of living water. [39 He said this about the Spirit which those who believed him inly were going to receive; for Spirit was not yet, because Jesus was not yet glorified.] 40 Some of the people, hearing these words, said, This is truly the prophet. 41 Others said, this is the Christ. But others said, Does the Christ come from Galilee? 42 Has not the scripture said that Christ comes out of the seed of David, and from Bethlehem, the village where David was? 43 So the crowd were divided over him; 44 some of them wished to arrest him, but no one laid hands on him.

45 The guards returned to the chief priests and Pharisees, who said, Why did you not bring him? 46 The guards replied, Never a man spoke as this man speaks. 47 The Pharisees retorted, Have you too been deceived? 48 Has any one of the rulers or of the Pharisees believed in him? 49 But this crowd, not Knowing the law, are cursed. 50 Nicodemus, who [had come to him at first, and] was one of them, says to them, 51 Does our law judge the man unless it first hears from him and knows what he does? 52 They answered, Are you also from Galilee? Search, and see that a prophet is not raised out of Galilee. 53 [And each went to his own house.]

Knowledge of the Divine is not possible through the head, where only luciferic beings speak, but through the rest of the organism. Mathematics, for example, is already experienced in the limbs. (Only the thought of the ego is experienced in the head.) We live primarily in our lower organism, our conscious-ness filled with desires — the digestive organs have been built up by the astral body living in the stomach. Today consciousness is rightly imbued with the desires of the astral body, which must be consciously developed.

The real 'I' does not enter the body, but is 'chained' to the solar plexus in the belly (*koilias*) — not the heart (*kardia*) as mis-translated. It works through the autonomic nervous system in all the lower bodily activities which culminate in the formation of blood. When we 'come to Christ' we can feel how this real cosmic 'I' stimulates the life forces in our digestion to rise to the heart. 'And when there is also a right understanding of Christ, the etherized blood rising from the heart to the brain meets together with the actual spiritualized bloodstream of Jesus Christ that flowed on Golgotha' (1.10.11). Through this blood the true ego aura comes into being.

At the autumn festival of Tabernacles (7:2), people had to visit daily a spring of flowing water to remind them of their spiritual nature and strivings; they drank in recollection. But not on the eighth day, the sabbath, when Jesus offered 'living water'. But we must 'die and become' before we can ascend through our own new forces, before 'rivers of living water' can flow from our belly to enkindle the spark of spiritual freedom, and bring the true ego to birth as healing spirit. Christ's sacrifice shows that people will be able to do this, for the Holy Spirit to appear. 'One follows Christ out of understanding and freedom, not out of contemplation of the Godhead. He does not come as a god working from above — without freedom, love is impossible' (18.4.09).

Christ could leave the body of Jesus and speak through one or other Apostle, and as their appearance was similar (p. 54) the guards could not know which one to arrest. But they perceived the power of the Word.

The 'I' Confronts Opposition

In reading this chapter we should emphasize the word 'I' or 'I am', and interpret it quite literally as the name of Christ. (It is mentioned 49 times here, 21 of them augmented by *ego*.) When he spoke the 'I', he did not refer just to himself but often to the higher self in everyone, the eternal universal ego, which is one with the spirit as foundation of the world. This is contrasted with the Jewish group soul.

And the Darkness did not take it in (1:5).

8:1–11 *The Adulteress — Sin and Destiny*

1 But Jesus went to the Mount of Olives. **2** At dawn he arrived again at the temple; [all the people came to him, and he sat down and taught them.] **3** The scribes and Pharisees bring a woman caught in adultery, and standing her in the midst **4** they say to him, Teacher, this woman has been caught in the act of adultery; **5** now in the law, Moses enjoined us to stone such; so what do you say? [**6** They said this tempting him, that they might have occasion to accuse him.] But Jesus stooped and inscribed with his finger in the earth. **7** As they remained questioning him, he straightened up and said, Let the sinless one among you throw at her the first stone. **8** And again stooping, he inscribed in the earth. **9** And hearing this, they went out one by one, beginning with the older ones; and he was left alone with the woman in the midst. **10** Straightening up, Jesus said, Woman, where are they? Did no one condemn you? **11** And she said, No one, sir. So Jesus said, Neither do 'I' condemn you; [go, do not sin again].

'Only a disciple initiated by Christ himself could have written this' (7.7.09) — either Lazarus/John, or the youth of Nain (Luke 7:11f) or the daughter of Jairus (Mark 5:42). Early manuscripts lack it, or place it elsewhere, and its style differs.

Christ bends to inscribe her deed into the earth, meaning that her eternal 'I' will compensate in a future life. (Knowledge of reincarnation was then almost universal except among the Semites and exoteric Christians – the esoteric always knew it.) He does not judge, but respects her 'I', and takes upon himself the objective effects of her deed on others. 'The individual must always bear the consequences for himself of his sin (though it will become necessary for this sometimes to be shared by the community), but cannot redeem its consequences for the World' (15.7.14). Each person can freely help one or more others: Christ helps all who allow his deed to work on them.

Sin arises from desires of the astral body; the task of the ego is to expiate it. Only if the sinner fills his soul with the active substance of the Being of Christ does the latter take the consequences on himself, and 'forgiveness of sins' is actually recognition that such is the case. He has taken over from the Cherubim the judgement of all human beings after death. Otherwise the sins remain as booty of Lucifer until Jupiter evolution.

Christ is the living incarnate earth karma, the living consciousness of the Akashic Record. He writes in occult script to generate in the Pharisees the right thought forms and to call forth the right deed. He then challenges them as to whether they are free from sin. For the first time they are thrown back on their own responsibility, not covered by the law. They could not know whether in a previous life they had influenced her or had sinned themselves, and so withdraw.

Christ teaches karma in practice, not as theory. The first impulse for developing the higher self thus flows into the earth. Unless reincarnation and karma are taught, physical humanity would be given over by Jehovah to a petrified earth, and the possibility of spiritualization given by Lucifer (representing the elemental Spirit Self) would be missed.

8:12–20 'I' Am the Light of the World* – My Judgement is True

12 Jesus spoke to them again, saying, 'I' am the light of the world; one who follows me will by no means walk in darkness, but will

---

* Second stage of development of the 'I am'.

have the light of life. **13** The Pharisees said, You witness to yourself; your witness is not valid. **14** Jesus replied, Even if 'I' witness concerning myself, my witness is true because I know whence I came and whither I go; but you do not know whence I come or whither I go. **15** You judge according to the flesh; 'I' do not judge anyone. **16** But even if 'I' judge, my judgement is true, because I am not alone, but 'I' and the one who sent me. **17** Even in your law it is written that the witness of two men is true. **18** 'I' am one who bears witness to myself, and there bears witness to me the Father who sent me. **19** They said, Where is your father? Jesus answered, You know neither me nor my Father. If you knew me you would also have known my Father. **20** He spoke these words in the treasury, teaching in the temple; and no one seized him, because his time had not yet come.

Were it not for the Fall, we should feel our ego or 'I am', the gift of the seven Elohim (Gen. 2:7) as sevenfold. Instead we must acquire this step by step. The first, given by Jehovah as the Law of Moses and abstract thinking (manna) must since the nineteenth century be superseded. 'The second, the Light of the World or spiritual insight, brought by the etheric Christ for our age, will bring healing, especially in a social context' (7.12.18). Without the radiant Being of Christ, our bodies would already decay even faster than they do. The primal Light (1:9) appears again in the light brought by Christ to the human ego; certainty of spirit and soul flourish again. That which can truly say 'I am' is literally the force of the Light of the World penetrating through space.

Normally we do not see light itself, only its effect. The Sun Being is now on earth. 'Since ancient Persia the sun cannot radiate light; physically it just reflects the light radiated by the regular planets towards it. Later it also became the reflector of life and love' (6.11.21). But in the sixth age, now in preparation, the higher self begins to see the light itself, which in this region is the element of life, and which is actually love – the warm being of the Logos streaming in the sunlight directly into mankind as guide for the Spirit Self. The light of Lucifer was raised by Christ to love. And in the later sixth main epoch (seals – Rev. 6) this light will become the source of a new sun, shining forth out of inner heart radiance. We must literally find this light within ourself as our eternal foundation. In the treasury the great candles were lit for the festival.

It is what we do during life on earth that 'judges' our future to come. Moral judgement follows cosmic law, which flows from the relationship between planets and constellations. Only since the 'I' became free in the twentieth century has it been possible for Christ as Lord of Karma to determine the balance of our karmic account after our death.

8:21–36 Raise Up the Son of Man — The Truth Will Set You Free

21 He said to them again, 'I' go, and you will seek me, and you will die in your sin; where I go you cannot come. **22** The Jews said, Will he kill himself? For he says, 'Where 'I' go you cannot come.' **23** And he said, You are of the things below, 'I' am of the things above. You are of this world, 'I' am not of this world. **24** I said therefore that you will die in your sins; for if you do not believe that 'I' am, you will die in your sins. **25** So they said to him, Who are you? Jesus said, What I also said to you at the beginning. **26** I have much to speak and judge about you. But he who sent me is true, and I speak into the world the things I heard from him. **27** They did not know that he spoke to them of the Father. **28** So Jesus said, When you raise up the son of man, then you will Know that 'I' am; and that I do nothing from myself, but I speak these things as the Father taught me. **29** And he who sent me is with me; he did not leave me alone, because 'I' always do the things pleasing to him. **30** As he spoke thus, many believed him inly.

31 So Jesus said to the Jews [who had believed him], If you abide in my Word, you are truly my disciples, **32** and you will know the truth, and the truth will set you free. **33** They answered, We are seed of Abraham and to no one have we ever been enslaved. How can you say, You will become free? **34** Jesus replied, Truly I tell[s] you, everyone who sins is a slave [to sin]. **35** But a slave does not stay in the house for ever; the son remains for ever. **36** If therefore the son frees you, you will be really free.

The everyday ego is only an image in the astral world of the real 'I', which is spirit. As such it is entwined in the realm of sin, of the things below, whereas Christ must be sought in the realm of the higher self, of the things above (3:3). The individual ego is not alone, but should feel its direct union with 'our Father', not through the blood but 'in spirit and truth', through the Hierarchies. The time has come to recognize the Father substance in which the 'I' is rooted, but the Jews know only 'the God of Israel'. They need to find the son of man within them (Dan. 7:13), not only Abraham. The 'son of man', the spiritual or consciousness soul that few had then reached (p. 26) must then be raised to receive the Spirit Self. (This does not refer to the Crucifixion, Resurrection or Ascension, because the Jews still did not know.)

Christ rises to a consciousness not accessible to his persecutors—one cannot see the 'I' without doing so. The more that I realize that for everything I do I am accountable to Christ, the more his etheric form will become visible. Then humanity finds brotherhood in the spiritual life (as already in mathematics). This points to the Whitsun experience, the awakening of the Holy Spirit in each individual (the separate tongues of fire) enabling the understanding of Christ. 'The mission of Christianity is a brotherhood in the light of the one truth. What unites is the sum of wisdom; it need not be preached. One who sins against this universal spirit of truth and wisdom commits the great sin against the Holy Spirit' (21.3.07), which cannot be forgiven (Matt. 12:32).

The Jews were under Roman rule, though still retaining their religion; but they were also tied to the bloodstream, not spiritually free of the body.

8:37–47 Your Father the Devil—'I' Came from God

37 I know that you are seed of Abraham, but you seek to kill me because my Word finds no place in you. **38** What 'I' have observed with the Father, that I speak; and you do what you heard from your father. **39** They answered, Our father is Abraham. Jesus says, If you are children of Abraham, you would do the deeds of Abraham, **40** but now you seek to kill me, a man who has spoken to you the truth which I heard from God. This Abraham did not do. **41** You do the deeds of your father. They said, We were not born of fornication, we have one father, God. **42** Jesus said, If God was your father, you would have loved me; for 'I' came forth and have come from God; for not of myself have I come, but he sent me. **43** Why do you not understand what I speak? Because you cannot hear my Word. **44** You have as father the devil; and you will to do your father's desires. He was a murderer from the beginning, and stood not in the truth, because truth is not in him. When he lies he speaks out of his own nature, for he is a liar and the father of lies. **45** But because 'I' tell the truth, you do not believe me. **46** Who of you convicts me of sin? If I tell the truth, why do you not believe me? **47** He who is of God hears the words of God. Hence you do not hear because you are not of God.

Abraham had renounced all inspiration coming from within, and turned to sense perception of outer nature, to measure, number and weight, and to thoughts of the inherited physical brain. The perfect organization of the brain necessary for Jesus had to be physically inherited from him, and the turn from clairvoyance to the intellect was a necessity for humanity. But from nature Satan/Ahriman, the devil, the father of lies, enters the human soul (whereas Lucifer rises from within the soul). 'The individual 'I' must now be tempered inwardly in confrontation with evil—that is indeed the divine purpose of evil, which becomes widespread in our age and will continue for a long time; for in overcoming evil is developed the strongest good' (25.6.08).

8:48–59 Before Abraham Was, 'I' am—He Went Out of the Temple

48 The Jews answered, Do we not rightly say that you are a Samaritan, and have a demon? **49** Jesus answered, 'I' have no demon; but I honour my Father, and you dishonour me. **50** But 'I' seek not my glory; there is One who seeks it and judges. **51** Truly

I tell you, if anyone keeps my Word, he will never behold death. **52** The Jews said, Now we know that you have a demon. Abraham died, and the prophets; and you say, If anyone keeps my word he will never taste death. **53** Are you greater than [our father] Abraham, who died? And the prophets died. Whom do you make yourself out to be? **54** Jesus answered, If 'I' glorify myself, my glory is nothing. The one glorifying me is my Father, whom you say is your God. **55** You have not known him, but 'I' know him. If I said I do not know him, I should be a liar like you, but I do know him and keep his Word. **56** Your father Abraham was glad to see my day; and he saw and rejoiced. **57** So the Jews said, You are not yet fifty years old, and have seen Abraham? **58** Jesus said, Truly I tell[s] you, before Abraham came to be, 'I' am. **59** So they took up stones to throw at him. But Jesus was hidden, and went forth out of the temple, [going through the midst of them].

Jews sought to combat Lucifer by deadening the ego and preserving the old way to God through Abraham. Union with Abraham and the whole people could still be felt within the pure Jewish bloodstream, but not the 'I'. They thought Abraham was alive in Paradise (Luke 16:22f), but not that he still lived in the Jewish folk memory, where Christ met him during his descent. But as Word, Christ was present at the origin of time (1:1) long before Abraham, asserting the eternal reality of the 'I am', a drop of Father-substance that pulses throughout the cosmos and in which every 'I' is rooted. The words of v. 58 contain the living essence of Christian doctrine, through which we approach communion with Christ, and through him with the Father.

' "Going out of the temple" refers to the astral body leaving the physical, as in sleep but with full consciousness of the astral plane, which is not accessible to his persecutors. One cannot see the 'I' without doing so. This is not painless, but a tearing apart, and usually takes three days' (11:39) (19.2.06). The outer must become an exact image of the inner for the spirit to shine through it.

These last three sections may indicate the regions of Soul Light, Active Soul Force and Soul Life respectively.

The Eternal 'I'

Now that Jesus is 'out of the temple', the narrative passes onto the plane of Imaginative picture, Christ penetrates to 'the god in man', the higher self which passes through successive incarnations.

Man came to be (1:6).

9:1–7 The Man Born Blind (Sixth Sign) — The God in Him

1 Passing by, he saw a man blind from birth. **2** His disciples asked, Rabbi, who sinned, this person or his parents, that he was born blind? **3** Jesus answered, neither he nor his parents sinned, but that the deeds of the god in him might be made manifest. **4** We must do the work of him who sent me while it is day; night comes, when no one can work. **5** While 'I' am in the world, I am light of the world. **6** Having said this, he spat on the ground, made clay of the spittle, and put the clay on his eyes, **7** saying, Go, wash in the pool of Siloam (which means 'sent'). So he went and washed, and came back seeing.

The usual explanation that the man was blind so that Jesus could heal and show off the glory of God is unchristian. In those days and in the Old Testament the idea of an outer God in the 'next world' was unknown. They envisaged an earth God (p. 29), although actually it was only the higher self. Error and sin are objective; they have results in the cosmos. The blindness from birth was due to a fault of the ego brought from a previous incarnation. Christ first connects morality, a concern of the ego, with healing; but morality cannot affect the physical in one incarnation. His power in Jesus thus increases further, beyond a single life.

Whereas the restoration of sight was not then uncommon, the

complete gift of sight was unique. The eye was originally created by light working on the body, and Christ bore the Light of the World within him (8:12). 'By uniting the special life forces within his spittle, prepared in a specific way related to the forces of death, with the forces of the earth (his body), these can become a healing substance in the presence of Christ' (26.5.08). But such healing could only be performed while Christ was incarnated, or when he comes again.

9:8–23 Healing on a Sabbath—He is a Prophet

8 The neighbours and those who saw him before as a beggar said, Is this not the one who sat and begged? **9** Some said, This is he; others, No, but he is like him. He said, 'I' am. **10** So they asked, How then were your eyes opened. **11** He replied, The man called Jesus made clay and anointed my eyes and told me, Go to Siloam and wash. So going and washing, I saw. **12** They said, where is he? He says, I do not know. **13** They lead him to the Pharisees, he who was once blind. **14** It was a Sabbath, the day Jesus made clay and opened his eyes. **15** So again the Pharisees too asked him how he saw. He said, he put clay on my eyes, and I washed, and I see. **16** Some of the Pharisees said, This man is not from God, because he does not keep the sabbath. But others said, How can a sinful man do such signs? There was a division between them. **17** So they say again to the blind one, What do you say about him, since he opened your eyes. And he said, He is a prophet. **18** The Jews did not believe that he had been blind and saw, until they called his parents **19** and asked them, Is this your son, whom you say was born blind? Then how does he now see? **20** His parents replied, We know that this is our son, and that he was born blind. **21** But how he now sees, we do not know, nor do we know who opened his eyes; ask him, he is of age and will speak for himself. **22** His parents said this because they feared the Jews; for the Jews had already agreed that if anyone should acknowledge him to be Christ, he would be expelled from the synagogue. **23** That is why his parents said, He is of age, ask him.

What the man receives is the strength to heal himself from within his eternal 'I' (cf. 5:6–8). That is the ego that passes from one incarnation to another. When someone says 'I am' he lives in the will within the seed of his next incarnation (cf. 1:21, 18:25).

'Opened' implies that the eyes were sightless, not necessarily closed. A nerve channel must open from eye to brain, through which the astral body and ego can unite with the object.

9:24–41 Are We Also Blind? — The Question of Our Age

24 So they called a second time the man who had been blind and said, Give praise to God; we know that this man is sinful. **25** He answered, I do not know whether he is sinful; I know one thing, that having been blind I now see. **26** So they said, What did he do to you? How did he open your eyes? **27** He replied, I told you already, and you did not listen. Why do you want to hear again? Do you also wish to become his disciples? **28** They reviled him, and said, You are his disciple, but we are disciples of Moses. **29** We know that God has spoken by Moses, but we do not know where this fellow comes from. **30** The man responded, This then is the astonishing thing, that you do not know where he comes from, yet he opened my eyes. **31** We know that God does not listen to sinners, but if anyone worships God and does his will, he listens to him. **32** It has never ever been heard of, that anyone opened the eyes of one born blind. **33** If this person was not from God, he could not do anything. **34** They retorted, You were born wholly in sins, do you teach us? And they cast him out.

35 Jesus heard that they had cast him out, found him, and said, Do you believe in The Son of Man? **36** He replied, Who is he, sir, that I may believe in him? **37** Jesus said, You have seen him, and the one speaking with you is that man. **38** [And he said, I believe, sir; and he worshipped him. **39** Jesus said,] 'I' came into this world for judgement, that those who do not see may see, and ones who see may become blind. **40** Some of the Pharisees with him heard this and said to him, Are we also blind? **41** Jesus said, If you were blind, you would not have been sinful; but now that you say, We see, your sin remains.

The youth now responds with the confidence of the higher self. He speaks of Jesus first as a man (v. 11), then as a prophet (v. 17), then as one from God (v. 33) and finally worships him as The Son of Man (v. 38). The Pharisees' main concern is again not the healing but the breaking of their rules for the sabbath (v. 65). They should have recognized that he came to fulfil the mission of David — their mission — as Lord in the human individuality. They cast out the youth although they must know, but do not wish to be reminded, that Isaiah had thrice predicted the gift of sight as a deed of the Messiah (Isa. 29:18, 35:5, 42:7). But eventually some of them realize that there is another dimension to blindness, blindness to spiritual reality. This was necessary in evolution so that the individual ego could manifest in freedom. 'One follows Christ only out of understanding and freedom, not out of contemplation of the Godhead' (18.4.09).

The Lesser Mysteries

'This chapter expresses the three stages of John's "purification" or awakening on the astral plane, in preparation for his initiation on the plane of spiritland in the next' (19.2.06). Verse 41 echoes 1:15, and divides the Gospel into two parts, the first to be understood through the witness of the Baptist, and the second through that of the beloved disciple himself.

Sent from God (1:6).

10:1–10 'I' Am the Door* —Leading Out to Pasture

1 Truly I tell[s] you, he who does not enter the sheepfold by the door, but climbs in another way, is a thief and a robber; **2** but he who enters through the door is the shepherd of the sheep. **3** The doorkeeper opens to him, and the sheep hear his voice; and he calls his own sheep by name and brings them out. **4** When he has all his own out, he goes before them, and the sheep follow him because they know his voice. **5** They will never follow a stranger, but will flee from him, because they do not know the stranger's voice. **6** This allegory Jesus told them, but they did not understand what he was speaking to them. **7** So Jesus said again, Truly I tell[s] you, that 'I' am the door of the sheep. **8** All who came before me are thieves and robbers, but the sheep did not heed them. **9** 'I' am the door; if anyone enters through me he will be saved, and will go in and out and will find pasture. **10** The thief comes only to steal and slaughter and destroy; 'I' came that they may have life, and may have it abundantly.

Those who lived before Jesus entered the soul-spiritual world through an atavistic clairvoyance that was and is no longer valid. 'When there is a special craving to enter, the person at the

---

* Third stage of development of the 'I am'.

Threshold pilfers, partakes stealthily, and this is densified by Ahriman to hallucinations, illusions. These may contain true pictures of the spiritual world, but not the important part, namely a clear view of the truth and of the value of what is seen' (31.8.13). Judas is called a thief (12:6) and Barabbas a robber (18:40).

'Enter' meant to look back inwards through the senses – the 'door of man' (Matt. 7:13). In studying thus the inner organs we come into contact with our pre-earthly existence – the true meaning of the Greek 'know yourself' – and experience in direct astral vision the Christ forces then raying down through the cosmic eye of the sun. First we must learn to move in and out in full consciousness.

Today however that inner core – our ego – is no longer there, only a reflection in the astral body of our pre-natal ego; it is in fact around us. Only when we meet another person does some impulse of our ego enter consciousness. So we must now seek instead beyond space and time the gate of nature-forms, whose forces enable us to make something of ourselves in freedom. This is the new Saturn path of initiation, based on Imaginative insight into the separate bodily organs. 'Such a spiritual anatomy leads to the corresponding creative forces in the cosmos (e.g. 6:26), which comprise an outer cosmic human being' (Torquay 21/ 2.8.24).

10:11-21 'I' Am the Goodly Shepherd* – Laying Down the Soul-life

11 'I' am the goodly shepherd. The goodly shepherd lays down his soul-life for the sheep. 12 The hireling who is not a shepherd, whose sheep are not his own, sees the wolf coming and leaves the sheep and flees, and the wolf seizes and scatters them; 13 for he is a hireling, and the sheep do not matter to him. 14 'I' am the goodly shepherd, and I Know mine, and mine Know me, 15 as the Father Knows me and I Know the Father; and I lay down my

---

*Fourth stage of development of the 'I am' (the higher ego).

soul-life for the sheep. **16** And I have other sheep which are not of this fold; those also I must bring, and they will hear my voice, and there will come to be one flock, one shepherd. **17** The Father loves me because 'I' lay down my soul-life, that I may take it again. **18** No one took it from me, but 'I' lay it down of myself. I have authority to lay it down and I have authority to take it again; this command I received from my Father. **19** There was again a division among the Jews because of these words. **20** Many of them said, He has a demon, and raves; why do you listen to him? **21** Others said, These are not the words of someone possessed by a demon. Can a demon open the eyes of the blind?

In the elemental soul world it is necessary to transform oneself in a high degree to resemble and be within the other being or process, hence we must lose the consciousness 'I am myself'. There comes a moment (as between death and rebirth) when all that one remembers disappears. It returns, but in an altered manner that shows what it must become. Unless we are ready to lay down (under Christ's guidance) all that belongs to the life of the soul, the lower self, it is not possible to receive the spirit. 'We must really leave behind all that we have experienced or acquired in our various incarnations before entering the world where this has no further meaning' (27.8.12). This emptied consciousness is then filled with the first spiritual member of our being, the astral body. Otherwise we shall be filled with terror and fear such that we cannot bear it. This is the meeting with the Guardian of the Threshold (see further Rudolf Steiner, *A Way of Self-Knowledge*, meditation 4).

When we 'take it again' in Imagination, what we then see is nothing but our own soul, and we must learn to suppress this before we can experience the objective spiritual world—our ordinary 'I' alone is retained in consciousness. It is just that which one has been that remains first in the spiritual world.

In Mark 10:18 Jesus specifically rejects being called 'good', which applies to God alone. *Kalos* means 'beautiful' (or 'goodly'), not good; but Hebrew had only one word for both. Beauty is the outward reflection of inner spirituality; feeling is raised to the divine.

10:22–42 'I' and the Father are One—You are Gods

22 It was the feast of Dedication in Jerusalem; **23** it was winter; and Jesus was walking in the temple in Solomon's colonnade. **24** The Jews surrounded him and said, How long will you keep our soul in suspense? If you are Christ, tell us plainly. **25** Jesus answered, I told you, but you do not believe. The deeds 'I' do in my Father's name testify to me; **26** but you do not believe because you are not of my sheep. **27** Mine heed my voice, and I Know them, and they follow me; **28** 'I' give them eternal life and they shall never perish, and no one shall snatch them out of my hand. **29** My Father, in what he has given to me, is greater than all, and no one has power to snatch them from my Father's hand. **30** 'I' and the Father are one. **31** The Jews again picked up stones to stone him. **32** Jesus responded, I showed you many fine deeds of the Father; for which of these deeds do you stone me? **33** The Jews replied, we do not stone you for a fine deed but for blasphemy, because, being a man, you make yourself God. **34** Jesus answered, Is it not written in your law: 'I' said, you are gods? **35** If he with whom was the word of God called them gods (and scripture cannot be broken), **36** do you tell him whom the Father consecrated and sent into the world 'you blaspheme' because I said, son of God am I? **37** If I do not do my Father's work, do not believe me; **38** but if I do, even if you do not believe me, believe the deeds, that you may Know and understand that the Father is in me, and 'I' in the Father. **39** So they tried again to arrest him, and he went forth out of their hand.

40 And he went away again across Jordan to the place where John first baptized, and remained there. **41** And many came to him and said, John indeed did no sign; but all the many things that John said about this person were true. **42** And many there had confidence in him.

The soul in every personality must become able to feel one with the eternal Ground of Worlds whom we call 'our Father'. This requires every night a decision of will to obliterate egoism and all the detailed memory of all that one has been—a most terrifying experience that one must approach with utmost confidence. 'Only then can the *true "I"* which is one with the Father be brought to us out of the cosmos, of which the physical ego is but the faintest shadow' (30.8.13). Here Christ is saying, 'I lay down my ego power, and receive the Father into myself (v. 30), that the primal principle may flow through me into others.'

The unity of Son and Father is reflected in the fact that the sun is also a star in the galaxy. With our 'I' we stand beyond the world of the stars, beyond the zodiac. The concept of the Trinity means that also 'I' and Holy Spirit are one. The physical body is bestowed by the Father, but through Christ we may partake of it.

In Psalm 82:6 God spoke to rulers and priests: 'You are gods, you are all sons of the Most High, but you will die like men.' These words are a wonderful guiding light. Lucifer said 'you shall be like god' (Gen. 3:5), but in the sun sphere after death we hear, 'you should be a god'. The former is a curse, the latter a blessing—it all depends on who speaks. Everyone is a divine spark of the cosmos, but it must be kindled.

The Initiation of Lazarus

This central chapter is the transition from the old mysteries of the Spirit to the new mysteries of the Son, the central subject of which is death and its transformation. 'In Christ we die.' Now the pupil has to fulfil in reality the words 'Die and Become'.

This is the seventh 'sign'.

Whose name was John (1:6).

11:1-16 Lazarus is Ill—To Manifest the Son of God

1 'Now a certain person was ailing, Lazarus from Bethany, the village of Mary and her sister Martha. [2 It was Mary who anointed the Lord with ointment and wiped off his feet with her hair, whose brother Lazarus was ill.] 3 So the sisters sent to him, saying, Lord, he whom you love is ill. 4 Hearing this, Jesus said, This illness is not unto death, but for the revealing of the god, that the son [of god] may be manifested through it. 5 Now Jesus loved Martha and her sister and Lazarus. 6 So when he heard that he was ill, he stayed where he was for two days.

7 After this time he says to the disciples, Let us go into Judea again. 8 They say, Rabbi, the Jews were seeking just now to stone you, and will you go there again? 9 Jesus answered, Are there not twelve hours in a day? If anyone walks by day he does not stumble, because he sees the light of this world; 10 but if anyone walks by night he stumbles, because the light is not in him. 11 Then he said, Our friend Lazarus has fallen asleep; but I'm going to awaken him. 12 The disciples said, Lord, if he has fallen asleep he will recover. 13 Now Jesus had spoken of his death, but they thought he spoke of the sleep of slumber. 14 So then Jesus told them plainly, Lazarus died; 15 and I rejoice because of you that I was not there, that you may believe. But let us go to him. 16 So Thomas, called the Twin, said to his fellow disciples, Let us also go, that we may die with him.

Martha and Mary represent the earthly and divine consciousness of Lazarus, sentient soul and intellectual soul
respectively. That part of Lazarus is ill into which the new man
permeated by the Word is to enter. Although for a long time
Jesus had made all ready, the death took place naturally without
him — this 'self-starting' quality is transitional to modern initiation. Instead of the etheric body dispersing as at natural death, it
was held sufficiently to maintain the physical, while Christ
poured into him his own impulse — it was a real symbol, not a
token — and he would be sure of the outcome. 'His purpose was
not to display "the glory of God" by a miracle, but to reveal the
god in Lazarus, and thus lead humanity to an understanding of
the Mystery of Golgotha' (CMF8). The disciples have as yet no
concept of initiation. Thomas represents the second (Persian) age
which is ready to be raised by Christ during the sixth age.

11:17–32 'I' Am the Resurrection and the Life[*] — The Fourth Day

17 When Jesus came, he found that he had already been four
days in the tomb. **18** Bethany was less than two miles from
Jerusalem, **19** and many Jews had come to Martha and Mary, to
console them over their brother. **20** So when Martha heard that
Jesus was coming she met him, while Mary sat in the house. **21**
Martha said to Jesus, Lord, if you had been here my brother
would not have died. **22** I know that even now whatever you ask
from God, God will give you. **23** Jesus says to her, your brother
will rise again. **24** Martha says, I know that he will rise again in
the resurrection on the last day. **25** Jesus said, 'I' am the Resurrection and the Life; he who trusts in me will live, even if he
should die, **26** and everyone living and trusting in me never dies;
do you believe this? **27** She says, Yes, Lord, 'I' am convinced that
you are the Christ, the Son of God, who is coming into the world.
28 Saying this, she went and called her sister Mary, saying privately, The Teacher is here and calls you. **29** When she heard this

---

[*] Fifth stage of development of the 'I am'.

she rose quickly and came to him. **30** Jesus had not yet come into the village, but was still where Martha met him. **31** The Jews with her in the house consoling Mary, seeing her get up quickly and go out, followed her, thinking that she was going to the tomb to wail. **32** When Mary came to where Jesus was, seeing him, she fell at his feet saying, Lord, if you had been here my brother would not have died.

'Whereas baptism was only a momentary immersion, Lazarus was in the tomb for 3½ days, as in the ancient mysteries. During the first day, he experienced in astral reality the first impulse for brotherhood at the transition from the third age, when the Father was still active in the blood and Moses experienced the "I am the I am", to the fourth age. He also formed a special link with the deceased Baptist, who penetrated him down to the spiritual soul, and through whom he saw the earlier chapters of the Gospel and understood who Jesus Christ actually was. On the second day he experienced the change to our present age, when man descends into matter to become in freedom a bearer of the 'I'. And on the third day he experienced how the spiritual soul is to be prepared by anthroposophy for the transition to the sixth age, through the common receipt of Spirit Self to a certain degree, and in a spiritual understanding of Christianity' (30.5.08, 28.9.24).

Lazarus was so advanced that he could receive from Christ an impulse strong enough to influence the circulation of his blood (p. 58), so that he could be initiated while still within the physical body. We must take verse 25 literally. The Word, the primordial power which flows from Christ and rises anew in Lazarus, *is* life that is eternal; he pours out the tidings of his own existence. The body has really been dead, but the eternal Word is brought to life in him.

11:33–44 Lazarus is Raised from the Dead (Seventh Sign) — Come Forth!

33 When Jesus saw her weeping, and the Jews coming with her weeping, he was deeply moved in spirit, and himself troubled.

34 He said, where have you laid him? They say, Lord, come and see. **35** Jesus shed tears. **36** So the Jews said, Look how he loved him. **37** But some of them said, Could not he who opened the eyes of the blind have even ensured that this one should not die? **38** Jesus, again deeply moved in himself, comes to the tomb — it was a cave, and a stone lying across it. **39** Jesus says, Lift the stone. Martha, the sister of the one who had died, says, Lord, by now he smells, for it is the fourth day. **40** Jesus says to her, Did I not tell you that if you have confidence, you will see the manifestation of the god? **41** So they lifted the stone. And Jesus lifted up his eyes and said, Father, I thank thee that thou hast heard me. **42** 'I' knew that thou always hearest me, but I said it because of the crowd standing around, that they may believe that thou hast sent me. **43** Having said this, he cried out with a loud voice, Lazarus, come forth! **44** The one who had died came out, his feet and hands bound with grave bands, and his face with a kerchief bound round it. Jesus says to them, Loosen him, and let him go.

Only on the fourth day was Christ physically present, to ensure that these astral experiences were properly impressed on the etheric body to be brought to consciousness, and that reconnection with the physical body was correctly made. The tears express that his 'I' strives to express more than otherwise possible, which presses the astral body together and contracts the physical, pressing out the tears. 'Come forth' and 'Let him go' are the traditional awakening calls of the mysteries, the hierophant's confirmation that henceforth the pupil works independently as an initiate, an arisen one. Though old forms were partly retained, Lazarus became an initiate in the new sense — a true transition. He has learned how initiation is attained. The spirit that as inner fire flows into his blood is a true Christian initiation with spirit and fire in the highest sense (Matt. 3:11). Only Christ could implant those forces which make Christian initiation possible.

The whole process leads to the revelation (not 'glorification') of the Godhead within Lazarus. There would be no point if he was the same as before. The eternal Word of the Father that existed in the beginning has risen in him, and the Father has heard. Christ is the resurrection for him here and now, and is the life that he then leads. His higher self is raised in a unique Fishes initiation to make him a son of God.

Note Part of a letter[*] from Clement of Alexandria (AD 150–211) quotes from and affirms that a secret version of Mark's Gospel was used in the church founded by Mark at Alexandria, which adds between Mark 10–34 and 10:35: 'And they come into Bethany, and a certain woman whose brother had died was there. And, coming, she prostrated herself before Jesus and says to him, "Son of David, have mercy on me." But the disciples rebuked her. And Jesus, being angered, went with her into the garden where the tomb was, and straightway a great cry was heard from the tomb. And going near, Jesus rolled away the stone from the door of the tomb. And straightway, going in where the youth was, he stretched forth his hand and raised him, seizing his hand. But the youth, looking upon him, loved him, and began to beseech him that he might be with him. And going out of the tomb, they came into the house of the youth, for he was rich ... '

This passage 'was read only to those being initiated into the greater mysteries'. It may be based on a recollection by Peter, whom Mark served while Peter was imprisoned in Rome. See further on p. 82. Lazarus had been rich, but had given up 'all that he had' (p. 5).

11:45–57 *The Jews Resolve on His Death—Not Only for the Nation*

45 Many of the Jews who had visited Mary and had seen what he did believed in him; **46** but some went to the Pharisees and told them what Jesus did. **47** So the chief priests and Pharisees assembled a Council and said, What are we to do, because this man does many signs. **48** If we leave him like this, [everyone will believe in him, and] the Romans will come and take from us both the place and the nation. **49** But one of them, Caiaphas, who was high priest that year, said to them, You know nothing, **50** and

---

[*] Morton Smith, *Clement of Alexandria and a Secret Gospel of Mark*, Harvard 1973.

don't realize that it is expedient for us that one man should die [for the people] and not all the nation perish. **51** He did not say this from himself, but being high priest that year he prophesied that Jesus was about to die for the nation; **52** and not only for the nation, but also that he might gather into one the children of God who were scattered. **53** From that day therefore they took counsel to kill him. **54** Jesus therefore no longer went about openly among the Jews, but went away into the country near the desert, to a town called Ephraim, and stayed there with the disciples.

55 Now the Jewish Passover was near, and many went up from the country to Jerusalem before Passover to purify themselves. **56** They looked for Jesus, and said to one another standing in the temple, what do you think? Surely he will not come to the feast? **57** Now the chief priests and Pharisees had given orders that if anyone knew where he was, he should inform, so that they might arrest him.

Jesus has deliberately revealed the mysteries in public and, as the Jews have no insight that the time for change has come, there can be no question but that according to law he must be put to death. That is the real reason behind their determination to crucify him.

Before the Last Supper, Lazarus joined the Twelve in place of John Zebedee, who was not a real Apostle but one with James, each representing an aspect of the intellectual or feeling-mind soul. He will now as an initiate bear the sacred name of John.

Last Days

After being in the spirit it is necessary to return to everyday life (10:9). The 'I' only reappears towards the end of this section.

He came as Witness (1:7).

12:1–11 The Anointment—To the Day of My Burial

1 Six days before the Passover, Jesus came to Bethany where Lazarus was, [whom Jesus had raised from the dead]. 2 They made supper for him there, and Martha served, while Lazarus was one of those reclining with him. 3 Mary, taking twelve ounces of costly ointment of pure spikenard, anointed the feet of Jesus, and wiped his feet with her hair; and the house was filled with the scent of the ointment. 4 Judas Iscariot, the one of his disciples who was about to betray him, says, 5 Why was this ointment not sold for a year's wages, and given to the poor? 6 He said this, not because the poor mattered to him, but because he was a thief, and having the box, used to lift what was put in it. 7 Jesus said, Let her alone, that she may keep it to the day of my burial; 8 for the poor you always have with you, but me you do not always have.

9 The great crowd of Jews knew that he was there, and came not only because of Jesus, but also to see Lazarus whom he raised from the dead. 10 But the chief priests took counsel to kill Lazarus too, 11 because on account of him many of the Jews left, and trusted in Jesus.

Mary may be the woman who probably washed, anointed and wiped the feet of Jesus before (Luke 7:38–8:2), when her sins were forgiven (her astral body purified). Now it must be seen as an embalming in advance of his death within a week. 'Jesus had to be anointed—purified and sanctified—to be proof in advance against whatever might approach his ego from the physical world before his ascension to sun and stars' (7.9.10). Moreover his body was already on the verge of dissolution because of the mighty power of Christ within it, which now held it together. The anointment points to the spirit which can enter the ego and stream forth from it again, an essential process. Four days later Jesus was anointed on the head at the house of Simon the leper (Mark 14:3-9).

Spikenard, also known as 'life of man', was used as a foot poultice for dropsy (fluid in tissues), and also against pain, flatulence and as a stimulus for heart and lungs—the quantity was huge. Care of feet was a servant's task; Mary humiliates herself by uncovering her hair to perform a necessary service.

Note The secret text of Mark recorded by Clement (p. 79) continues: 'And after six days Jesus told him what to do, and in the evening the youth comes to him wearing a linen cloth (*sindōn*) over [his] naked [body]. And he remained with him that night, for Jesus taught him the mystery of the Kingdom of God. And thence, arising, he returned to the other side of the Jordan.' At Mark 10:46 is added: 'And the sister of the youth whom Jesus loved and his mother and Salome were there, and Jesus did not receive them.'

The mysteries were indeed taught by night (3:2). That Jesus 'told him what to do' helps explain his part in the action at 13:25 and 18:12. This text suggests that 'the mystery of the Kingdom of God' is a step even beyond the initiation now given to Lazarus (perhaps the mystery of good and evil in the far future, set out in the book of Revelation, the mystery of the Father).

12:12-19 Entry into Jerusalem—Blessed is He

12 Next day the large crowd coming to the feast, hearing that Jesus was coming to Jerusalem, **13** took palm fronds and went out to meet him, crying, Hosanna, Blessed is he who comes in the name of the Lord, the King of Israel. **14** And Jesus found a young ass and sat on it, as it is written, **15** Fear not, daughter of Zion; behold thy king is coming, sitting on the colt of an ass. **16** His disciples did not understand this at first, but when Jesus was glorified they remembered that this was written of him, and had been done to him. **17** The people who had been with him when he called Lazarus out of the tomb and raised him from the dead bore witness. **18** The crowd also met him because they heard that he had done this sign. **19** So the Pharisees said to themselves, Look how you are getting nowhere, see, the world has gone after him.

Hosanna means 'save us, we beseech thee'. Meditation on the tones of the Hebrew sentence shows how the disciples are led towards maturity. The cry 'King of Israel' will influence Pilate (18:33, 19:19) because surrounding countries had been led by initiate kings.

'The colt was probably necessary because the last three years had been for Christ a continual process of slow death' (9.1.12), so that his physical strength was waning as he strove to die as mere human being. But in the mysteries the colt was another sign for Cancer, and it marks a leap in the development of the disciples. Christ stood spiritually at the summit of his spiritual power; his sun stood at its zenith in Cancer, whose forces the disciples are to carry to mankind. These are the heart forces, through which 'selflessness leads to purification'. (Zech. 9:9.)

12:20–26 The Grain of Wheat—He who Hates his Soul

20 Now among those going up to worship at the feast were some Greeks. **21** These approached Philip from Bethesda in Galilee and asked, Sir, we wish to see Jesus. **22** Philip tells Andrew, and together they tell Jesus. **23** Jesus answers, The hour has come that the Son of Man is glorified. **24** Truly I tell[s] you, unless the grain of wheat falls into the ground and dies, it remains alone; but if it dies, it bears much fruit. **25** He who loves his soul-life loses it, and he who hates his soul-life in this world will keep it unto eternal life. **26** If anyone serves me let him follow me, and where 'I' am, there will my servant be; if anyone serves me, the Father will honour him.

The Greeks wanted to see outwardly, but must learn to behold inwardly. Emotionally more objective than the Jews, they can well understand the parable—only one who hates his soul will wish to change it and thus progress (10:17–18).

Jesus consistently refers to himself as 'son of man', not 'son of god'. The spirit does not die—it is eternal life.

12:27–36 *The Ruler of this World Cast Out—Trust in the Light*

27 Now has my soul been troubled, and what may I say? Father, save me from this hour? But for this I came to this hour. 28 Father, glorify Thy name! Then came a sound from heaven: I both have glorified it, and will glorify it again. 29 The crowd who stood and heard it said that there was thunder; others said, An Angel has spoken to him. 30 Jesus replied, This voice has happened not because of me but for your sakes. 31 Now is the judgment of this world; now shall the ruler of this world be cast out. 32 And 'I', if I am lifted up out of the earth, will draw everyone towards myself. 33 This he said to signify by what kind of death he was about to die. 34 The crowd answered, We heard from the law that the Christ remains forever; how can you say that the son of man must be lifted up? Who is this son of man? 35 So Jesus said, Yet a little while the light is among you. Walk while you have the light, lest darkness overtakes you; he who walks in darkness does not know where he is going. 36 While you have the light, trust in the light, that you may become sons of light. This Jesus said, and going away was hidden from them.

Christ now felt anguish like a human being, and all power had departed from him. Out of this suffering came the all-prevailing cosmic love.

'The casting out of "the ruler of this world" (Lucifer as well as Ahriman) from the physical body of Jesus was necessary in so far as he had succumbed to the third Temptation, in order that his physical/etheric body should revert to its state before the Fall. Through the "glorify (or reveal) thy name" the etheric body of Jesus was so transformed by Christ that in the fullest sense it could impart new life to the physical—the sound was audible only to those duly prepared' (5.7.09).

The restoration of the physical phantom (p. 87) undertaken by Christ during the three years since the Baptism had provided the necessary foundation for the descent of the 'I'. Now even a few non-initiates endowed with the 'I' through natural powers experienced within the 'I' the radiant Son principle as the great healer also of the physical body that was beginning to crumble.

12:37–50 *Isaiah Said—I Have Come as Light*

37 Though he had done so many signs before them, they did not believe him inly; **38** that the word of the prophet Isaiah might be fulfilled: 'Lord, who believed our report, and to whom was the arm of the Lord revealed?' **39** They could not therefore believe, because Isaiah said again, **40** 'He has blinded their eyes and petrified their heart, that they might not see with the eyes and understand with the heart; and might turn, and I will cure them.' **41** Isaiah said these things because he saw his glory and spoke with him. **42** Nevertheless many even among the rulers believed him inly; but because of the Pharisees they did not confess, lest they should be expelled from synagogue; **43** for they loved the praise of men more than the praise of God.

44 But Jesus called out, He who trusts in me entrusts himself not to me but to the One who sent me; **45** and he who beholds me beholds Him who sent me. **46** 'I' have come as [a] light into the world, that everyone trusting in me may not remain in darkness. **47** And if anyone hears my words and does not keep them, 'I' do not judge him; for I came, not to judge the world but to save the world. **48** He who rejects me and does not receive my words has his judge—the words I spoke will judge him on the last day. **49** For 'I' did not speak from myself, but the Father who sent me commanded what I may say and what I may speak. **50** And I know that his commandment is eternal life. What 'I' speak, therefore, I speak as the Father has said to me.

The quotations are from Isa. 53:1, 6:10 and 6:1 respectively. Whenever the prophets spoke of him who revealed himself spiritually they meant the Logos of whom John writes; whereas the words Father, Son and Holy Spirit were used exoterically in manifold ways, so that the real esoteric meaning might not be directly evident. Isaiah saw Christ, who was always to be seen in the spirit, and he spoke with (not of) him—he is the actual 'Spirit of God' of Genesis 1.

Interlude

Up to this point the Gospel has ostensively been concerned with the descent of Christ into Jesus and into earthly space and time, with his public ministry, and with the opposition that he met from the Jewish priesthood despite their foreknowledge of a coming Messiah. An important part was depicted through John the Baptist, who was twice mentioned even after his death.

The Evangelist says, Here on this earth Christ lived, he worked with divine occult powers, he healed the sick, he went through everything from death to resurrection. It is impossible to understand these things with the intellect, but it is possible to rise to higher worlds where one can find the wisdom to understand who was among us.

The Prologue not only sets the theme of Creation through the Word becoming Life and inner Light, but also outlines the structure of the first half of the Gospel. It is important to consider not only 'what' is said but also 'how' it is said; for it has no less an architectonic structure than a great cathedral or a classical symphony, interweaving varied themes which show a purposeful path of self-development.

We may first observe broadly that 2:25 (he knew what was in man) to 4:24 (worship in spirit and truth) are mainly concerned with the sense-nervous system, that 4:47 (cure his son) to 5:2 (the signs he did on the sick) concern healing and life processes, and 6:5 (where can you buy loaves) to 6:58 (eat this bread) concern the digestion. Then whilst 'in the temple' in Jerusalem this is impressed on the physical phantom in the metabolism (7:14–7:39), the rhythmic system (7:40–8:11) and the head (8:12–8:59), restoring the phantom from the effects of the Fall (p. 132).

The most obvious sequence is the seven episodes perceptible to the senses, some designated as 'signs', which are generally interpreted as 'miracles' similar to those reported by the synoptics. The miraculous is nothing other than the penetration of higher worlds into our own. Nicodemus recognized Jesus by the signs he was doing (3.2). The people asked, 'What signs do you do' (6:30), and he himself said, Even if you do not believe me, believe the deeds (10:38).

  These perceptible signs of Christ's growing earthly power are considered to be:

Marriage at Cana (2:1–11)	Raising of Lazarus (11:30–44)
Healing the Official's Son (4:43–54)	Healing the Man Born Blind (9:1–32)
Healing at the Pool (5:1–8)	Appearing on the Water (6:16–21)
Feeding of Five Thousand (6:1-15)	

These are all visual pictures, two-dimensional imaginations. What the author has described so far are experiences during his initiation, clothed in a narrative of external events. Being *astral* experiences (though imprinted on the etheric body) these are moreover experienced in reverse time sequence (during sleep the astral body works back over the previous day, after death we go back over our life). Such a retrospect always takes place at the transition to the soul world. The pupil is at first spiritually 'blind from birth' (9). He needs to free himself first from the group soul (spiritual heredity) and to recognize his 'I am' as eternal spirit (8). He will encounter confusion and the three beasts while 'in the temple' (7). But vision of Jesus 'across the water' brings spiritual nourishment (6), which leads to healing and understanding of karma (5) to a new form of worship (4), and to recognition of the Son of God (3). This leads to the cleansing of the 'temple', to marriage with the spiritual world (2) and finally to the Appearing of the Word from above and, ultimately, to its origin (1). This represents a practice of spirit remembering.

  With this are already interwoven the seven great 'I am' sayings, which point both to the inner nature of the Being of Christ and to the experiences which each human soul is called on to make real within his own 'I'. That is the gift of Christ within him:

'I'AM the Bread of Life (6:35)	—	'I'AM the True Vine (15:1)
'I'AM the Light of the World (8:12)		'I'AM the Way, the Truth and the Life (14:6)
	'I'AM the Door (10:7)	'I'AM the Resurrection and the Life (11:25)
	'I'AM the Goodly Shepherd (10:11)	

These are not visualizations but statements to be heard and affirmed, namely inspirations (one-dimensional). As experiences of spiritland they are only possible through 'laying down the soul and receiving it again' (10:18), and as such are no longer reversed. They start from bread, the product of physical work, followed by light, an etheric formative force, and by the door or Threshold to the astral world at which stands the Guardian. It is he who shepherds the soul to recognition of the true 'I' and its destiny. Then the forces of resurrection and life become the way to spiritual truth that bears fruit in spiritland as inspiration for future evolution. Thus the everyday I (4:26) grows to the higher eternal 'I' (6:20) and eventually to the true 'I' (8:58). It is a practice of spirit awareness.

John's own higher development in *spiritland* begins with the 13th Chapter, the outer events of which occur within 24 hours and in significance are beyond space and time. We shall see how he incorporates this into his narrative of events, which contains mighty seeds for future evolution. Only an initiate, not a clairvoyant, could have written this spiritual substance, whereas the Synoptic Gospels are the work of clairvoyants. The events themselves read like the memory of an eyewitness, and the beloved disciple was the only one of the Apostles present at the Crucifixion. Although not written down until decades later, such outstanding events must have left an indelible impression on an initiate who was awake to them at a time when memory was much stronger than today.

What follows is thus a description of the Christian path of initiation for the mind-soul age, which can still be lived through sentence by sentence. It really gives strength to an independent higher life. He who takes it as just an account of external happenings does not understand it.

Washing of the Feet (13:1)	Ascension
Scourging (19:11)	Entombment and Resurrection (19:42–20:14)
Crown of Thorns (19:12)	Death (19:30)
Crucifixion (19:18)	

These are situations of destiny to be lived through in future as the seven degrees of Christian initiation. They form the path to union of the true 'I' with the Father (10:30), but the seventh stage of 'Ascension' is reserved by John for his Apocalypse (Rev. 10:15ff.). Here he speaks instead of the gift of the Holy Spirit (20:22), the permeation of the entire astral body by Spirit-Self. The significance of these events will be considered in context.

What we now have before us is in reality a cosmic writing, a mighty tableau, whose meaning flows out of the pictures themselves. Every sentence can become a source of spiritual forces for everyone who really experiences it in such a way as to become one with it. Things may light up that we did not know before, helping us to realize the tasks immediately before us. We can become different beings. *'Any sort of comment or interpretation in abstract ideas may be far more of a hindrance than a help.* It is, above all, a matter of letting things work impartially upon one, it is not at all necessary to strive after becoming clairvoyant.

'When we enter the true spiritual world, we enter a world of living thought-beings; the sum total of these beings and their deeds is the many voiced, many toned Cosmic Word, rich in manifold activities. In this Cosmic Word we become accustomed to live with our resounding soul being, ourselves Cosmic Word, performing deeds in the spiritual world.' (27.8.13).

Christ himself did not undergo initiation. He was from the start already permeated through and through to the very highest degree with Divine self-consciousness. The power of Resurrection was already there at the time of the Baptism. He was himself an initiator, and was finally raised by the Father, not by any human hierophant.

If we recognize the laying down of soul life (10:17) in the context of the lesser mysteries, and the laying down of life (11:14) in that of the greater mysteries, we may recognize the further Mystery of Golgotha in its cosmic immensity.

PART TWO

The Last Supper

13:1–11 *The Washing of the Feet*

1 Now before the feast of the Passover, Jesus, knowing that his hour had come to depart out of this world to the Father, and loving his own in the world, he loved them to the end. **2** And during supper, the devil having already put it into the heart of Judas son of Simon Iscariot that he should betray him, **3** Jesus, knowing that the Father gave all things into his hands, and that he came from God and goes to God, **4** rises from the supper, puts aside his garments, and taking a towel tied it round himself. **5** Then he pours water into the basin and began to wash the disciples' feet, and to wipe off with the towel which he had tied round him. **6** So he comes to Simon Peter, who says to him, Lord, do you wash my feet? **7** Jesus: What 'I' am doing you do not yet know, but afterwards you will understand. **8** Peter: By no means shall you ever wash my feet. Jesus: Unless I wash you, you have no part with me. **9** Simon Peter: Lord, not only my feet, but also my hands and my head. **10** Jesus: One who has been bathed does not need to wash [except the feet], but is wholly clean; and you are clean, but not all. **11** For he knew the one betraying him, and that was why he said, You are not all clean.

John here describes his experiences with Christ in the world of the spirit, which every human being can inwardly experience when he expands himself into the universe around him. He who formerly descended through time (sevenfold) now pours into space (twelvefold). The transition from children of God (1:12) to brothers of Christ begins.

The setting is a Waterman (Mark 14:13) initiation house in Jerusalem — by tradition that of Joseph of Arimathea (19:38). The synoptics regard the occasion as the Passover meal, which theologians tend to support historically; but John sees it as part of a cosmic imagination in which the death of Jesus next day is the true killing of the paschal lamb. Washing feet was a servant's task, forbidden to disciples.

'This scene is not only an historical event, but also the transforming of an experience in the past mysteries of the Spirit into the future mysteries of the Son. When in past initiations the etheric body was loosened, each of the twelve parts of the body was experienced as a human figure, with the pupil himself as the soul of the twelve. The initiate felt these figures as twelve of his own lives or stages of consciousness' (1.4.07). The Essenes had such a mystic communion, a twelvefold humanity, with John the Baptist as the final figure. The scene relates to the primordial twelvefoldness surrounding Christ in the world of Providence (6:13).

It was necessary at this time that the etheric body should come right down into the material world. Fundamentally this has been the object of religious education for the last 2000 years. Peter, meaning 'rock', represents the part of the body directed to the earth; his feet must be purified (v. 8). It is not merely that Jesus set an example of extreme humility. Knowing that now all is in his hands (v. 3), he was aware that the future stages of human development depended on him. But there is a spiritual law that nothing can exist without the basis of that which is below it. Similarly Jesus Christ himself could not exist without the Twelve.

The first trial of Christian esoteric development for the mind-soul age prior to the fifteenth century was to experience this fully. After weeks or months of meditation on this law, the pupil saw what humanity must go through to the end of the earth. He then felt as though water laved his feet, and a mighty vision arose within him of washing the feet of twelve people sitting around him, and of Christ's deed. He also felt that his muscles were strengthened. But this path is now very hard to follow (List α, p. 147).

In the Rosicrucian-Christian path for the present spiritual soul age, this is replaced by the meditative study of spiritual science and its activation in life. We develop as precondition a purposeful, living thinking free of all sense perceptions (like mathematics), testing the thoughts of all humanity, and the feelings resound to the stupendous facts of the spiritual world. We become aware of the dependence of the individual 'I' upon the surrounding community (List β). Compare the situation of Johannes in Scene 1 of *The Portal of Initiation*.

13:12–20 He Who Ate My Bread

12 When he had washed their feet, taken his garments, and reclined again, he said, Do you Know what I have done to you? **13** You call me Teacher and Lord, and you speak rightly, for I am. **14** If therefore 'I', the Lord and Teacher, washed your feet, so ought you to wash the feet of one another. **15** For I gave you an example, that as 'I' did to you, you may also do. **16** Truly I tell[s] you, a servant is not greater than his lord, nor one who is sent greater than he who sent him. **17** If you understand these things, blessed are you [if you do them]. **18** I do not speak of you all; 'I' know whom I chose, that the scripture may be fulfilled: 'He who ate my bread lifted up his heel against me.' **19** I tell you now before it happens, so that when it happens you may believe that 'I' am. **20** Truly I tell[s] you, whoever receives anyone I may send receives me; and whoever receives me receives him who sent me.

Other religions were founded by a teacher, but Christ, as Cosmic 'I', poured himself into the earth as lord of the soul forces. He has descended to a physical body, the oldest and most perfect of the sheaths; the astral body, sinful and determined by natural urges and passions, is its servant, and needs to be purified.

'We are the servants, not the masters, of the higher forces in nature (Mark 9:35, 10:43). Without this experience we can have no true perception of the Christian mysteries. Similarly Christ sees the disciples as lords of the community out of which he has arisen. His mission will now depend on them' (13.2.06). Moreover they represent the stages of consciousness through which he passes, starting from the fifth (Old Semitic) age of Atlantis, when in an etheric body he brought blood-based love (mother-love) to newly conscious sexuality, and finishing with the second age of the sixth epoch, when the whole of his spirit will have been poured into the blood-warmth of individuals to form the great brotherhood of humanity in Life Spirit. To all these twelve stages of consciousness he must bring salvation — our age, for example, when the deepest dependence on the senses combines with the greatest egoism, the age of the Antichrist, is represented by Judas.

The scripture in v. 18 has no specific source. It does not just refer to Judas, who takes the morsel (v. 26). We lift our heel against the earth as we walk; only the earth itself can speak as Christ speaks here; he can do so because he is becoming gradually the Earth Spirit. He feels the whole human community resting on him, he feels under its heel (Ps. 41:9). All the bread, all material of the earth, is his flesh; all the juice, all the fluid is his blood (6:53–7). This is not just a ritual (Mark 14:22–4); the whole of the earth planet is thus sanctified. Our soul-spiritual nature is gradually united with the soul-spirituality of the earth which is Christ. He begins to flow through us; we feel him within us. Then our heart will be the most powerful organ in us. But he may also still be found without.

13:21–30 The Empowerment of Judas

21 Saying these things, Jesus was troubled in spirit, and testified, Truly I tell[s] you that one of you will betray me. 22 The disciples looked at one another, perplexed about whom he speaks. 23 One of his disciples, whom Jesus loved, was reclining in the lap of Jesus; 24 so Simon Peter nods to this one and says to him, Tell us who it is about whom he speaks. 25 Leaning back thus on the breast of Jesus, that one says to him, Lord, who is it? 26 So Jesus answers, It is the one to whom 'I' shall dip the morsel and give to him. So he takes the morsel, and dipping it gives it to Judas son of Simon Iscariot. 27 And after the morsel, Satan entered into that one. So Jesus says to him, What you do, do quickly. 28 But none of those reclining knew what he had told him. 29 Some thought that since Judas had the box, Jesus tells him, Buy things we need for the feast; or that he should give something to the poor. 30 So

having taken the morsel, He immediately went out; and it was night.

That Jesus was troubled suggests that he was again tempted to defer his death, but instead he affirmed it. From this flowed the greatest freedom and love. We must see in Jesus Christ one whose very nature was that of resignation.

The lap (*kolpos*) is literally the fold of the garment above the belt. We can imagine the beloved disciple to the right of Jesus, reclining with his left elbow on a cushion (seats were not used). To speak to Jesus he would need to bend his head back, close to the breast of Jesus. 'This gesture symbolizes the future transfer in the sixth age of the human creative forces from the sexual region to that of the heart, lungs and larynx, where reproduction will be effected through the word. It is an awakening on the plane of spiritland, and John is aware of this. He thus represents the creative heart forces, which are central to the mysteries of the Son' (2.12.06). He would have realized that Judas was about to betray Jesus, and have wanted to intervene, but saw that by giving the morsel Jesus was in control.

Matthew reports (26:25) that Judas responded by saying, Is it I, Master? Egoism, lower desire, is the betrayer. So his conscience was not yet killed. And the sharing of bread was a gesture of close fellowship, as if he might still be redeemed. Since 'I am the bread' (6:35), Jesus gives of himself to Judas. 'It were better for him if he was not born' (Mark 14:21); yet it was a necessary deed if a God was to experience death. 'In this context Judas appears not only as a traitor but also as a martyr — he was an organic part of Christ's mission. We see the earthly reflection of the opponents of the gods set in opposition to the gods by the gods themselves. This has meaning for the whole cosmos, by which the significance of the physical earth could be recognised' (14.11.11). The world has to take in a heaven made of something which came out of evil and its overcoming.

Judas was in his last life Judas Maccabeus (1 Macc. 2:66–9.19), who fought for Judaism with great energy, and made a treaty with Rome. He was still so bound up with Hebrew nationalism that he could not find the bridge to Christ — he had to put money, materialism, before spirit for one life, and thus represents our materialistic age. 'It is a real fact that Diabolos, the demons, took possession of Judas' (v. 27) (26.6.05). Through this the astral body was led downwards; it is the nadir of the Dark Age (Kali Yuga).

13:31–38 As I Loved You, Love One Another

31 So when he went out, Jesus says, Now was the son of man glorified; and in him God was glorified. **32** [If in him God was glorified,] God will both glorify him in him, and will glorify him immediately. **33** Children, yet a little while I am with you; you will seek me, and as I said to the Jews I also say to you now, that where 'I' go you cannot come. **34** A new commandment I give you, that you love one another; that as I loved you, you also love one another. **35** By this everyone will know that you are my disciples, if you have love among one another.

36 Simon Peter says to him, Lord, where are you going? Jesus: Where I go, you cannot follow me now, but you will follow later. **37** Peter: Lord, why cannot I follow you yet? I will lay down my soul for you. **38** Jesus: Will you lay down your soul for me? Truly I tell you, a cock will not crow until you deny me three times.

Jesus speaks first of the beloved disciple, who has newly joined the Twelve. As a 'son of man' he had already been glorified (awakened, 11:43) to 'son of God' (Spirit Self) according to the old Mysteries of the Spirit (modified). This god in him now glorifies (spiritualizes) him further in the immediate moment to Life Spirit, through the gesture from lap to heart (v. 25). This is John's further initiation into the Mystery of the Son.

At this point the synoptics describe the institution of the Eucharist (Mark 14:22–25). But John has already emphasized the importance of giving thanks (6:11, 6:26), and has spoken of 'eating my flesh' and 'drinking my blood' (6:53); and now he has sanctified all earthly substance by characterizing Christ as Spirit of the Earth (v. 18). It was the juice of the grape, not fermented wine, of which Jesus said, This is my blood. Bread and wine are the symbol of the fourth age.

'Love your neighbour as yourself' had been law (Lev. 19:18) since Moses in the fifteenth century BC, but this was within the bloodstream. Then the Buddha brought the teaching of universal compassion in the sixth century BC. 'Now Christ brings just one new commandment to his Children: Love one another "as I loved you". This is not just a feeling but the cosmic power of love, based on the 'I' which overflows in sacrifice, a deed of the heart. Such love is first fully possible for the wholly independent 'I'' (20.5.08); only now can the Gospel speak of it. The self will be able to love in the spirit of Michael without loving itself, and on this path Christ can be found. For the etheric body is the same as the body of love. To love what is around us with brother-love is to follow Christ; so we may say 'Christ is the first of many brothers'. The very mission of the earth is the cultivation of the principle of love to its highest degree.

Peter—half asleep since the shock of the Transfiguration (Mark 9:2)—is so upset by the news of Jesus' departure that he sidesteps the new commandment. Commitment of soul (*psyche*), affirmation not denial, must precede commitment of life (10:17).

The Last Discourse

14:1–7 'I' Am the Way, the Truth and the Life[*]

1 Let not your heart be troubled; [you] believe in God, believe in me also. **2** In my Father's house are many abodes; otherwise I would have told you: [for] I go to prepare a place for you. **3** And should I go and prepare a place for you, I will come again and receive you to myself, that where 'I' am, you may also be. **4** And where 'I' go, you know the way. **5** Thomas says, Lord, we do not know where you are going, how do we know the way? **6** Jesus says, 'I' am the way, and the truth, and the life; no one comes to the Father except through me. **7** If you had Known me, you would also have Known my Father. Henceforth you Know him, and have seen him.

This chapter is based on questions by individuals, typical of the consciousness soul in our age (e.g. Parzival), and on understanding through the spirit. It concerns the step from the everyday ego to the spiritual reality of the higher 'I' outside the body.

After death the different peoples work on nature to build the 'house' in which they will later reside. The Father's house is the Earth itself. At the first stage of initiation the initiate must become a 'homeless person', that is, with no special sympathies or antipathies; and then he must build for himself a home on the other side, beyond space and time. The 'son of God' or Spirit Self is to be found in one's relationship to those around one; into this hollow space Christ may enter. 'Christ thus prepares the place for every "I" to build its own dwelling "where I am", i.e. in community, "where two or three are gathered together", yet all are united in the Christ principle' (8.3.07).

Doubting Thomas, the melancholic who thinks only physi-

---

[*] Sixth stage of development of the 'I am'.

cally, wants to know, but does not understand. Religious leaders such as Elijah have shown the way, Moses taught the truth, but only Christ, the embodiment of the Logos, can say, 'I' am the Life (1:4). He had already expressed this in Imaginative form to Peter, James and John—pupils of the second degree—at the Transfiguration (Mark 9:2f). Now that he has raised the eleven to a meditative consciousness, he expresses it verbally to them all in the sixth great 'I am' statement expounded below—the way (v. 12), the truth (v. 17) and the life (v. 19).

'The first task of the 'I' is to transform the astral body into Spirit Self, the nature of which is truth; the next will be, with Christ's help, to transform the etheric body, with its temperament and memories, into Life Spirit. These are the two trees of Paradise, of which we received originally only that of knowledge, because only through the 'I' can one come to the life of Christ' (15.2.09). The third task will be to transform the physical body into Spirit Man, the realm of the Father. But we can only work on the physical through the etheric formative forces: hence 'no one comes to the Father except through me'; to know one is to know the other. 'The childhood forces of walking upright, speaking and thinking, originally under the guidance of the Hierarchies, must now be brought to consciousness as the "son of God"' (25.2.11).

Jesus goes to his death, and we have all died many times, so that we all know in our higher self the way to spiritland: In Christo Morimur (In Christ we die).

14:8-21 *The Counsellor*

8 Philip says, Lord, show us the Father, and we shall be satisfied. 9 Jesus says, I am with you for such a long time, and have you not known me, Philip? He who has seen me has seen the Father; how can you say, Show us the Father? 10 Do you not believe that 'I' [am] in the Father, and the Father is in me? The words that 'I' say to you I do not speak from myself, but the Father who abides in me does his works 11 Believe me, that 'I' in the Father and the Father in me; or else, believe because of the works themselves. 12 Truly I tell[s] you, one who believes me inly will also do the

deeds that I do, and he will do greater than these because 'I' go to the Father; **13** and whatever you ask in my name, this I will do, that the Father may be revealed in the Son. **14** If you ask [me] anything in my name, 'I' will do it. **15** If you love me, you will keep my commandments.

16 And I will request the Father, and he will give you another Counsellor, that he may be with you forever, **17** the Spirit of Truth, whom the world cannot receive because it neither beholds nor knows him; you know him, because he abides with you and will be in you. **18** I will not leave you orphans, I am coming to you. **19** Yet a little while and the world no longer beholds me, but you behold me; because 'I' live, you too will live. **20** In that day you will Know that 'I' in my Father and you in me and I in you. **21** He who has my commandments and keeps them is the one who loves me, and the one who loves me will be loved by my Father, and I will love him and reveal myself to him.

Philip, the sanguine, represents the Greeks (12:21), who always wanted to see the beauty of their gods visible in the temple (the temptation of Lucifer). He is enjoined to progress inwardly from perception (8) through belief (11,12) to love (15,21). But to transform the astral body rightly, belief must be supported by true understanding of the spirit. If faith is nourished by the truths of anthroposophy, Spirit Self will arise of itself from the astral body. This concerns the transfiguration of the head. The concept of mutual indwelling (12:45) is emphasized by the absence of the copula in vv. 10,11,20.

'The Father does not work as cosmic mind and never will do' (8.3.07). He stands behind everything that lives in form, that can be perceived by the senses, that we alter by our actions. And he is specifically the spirit of common origin of bodies and souls, the uniting principle in each of us, 'our Father'. The Father Spirit, the spirit of common origin, must enter into our individual selves. As such he can be reached by thinking. But in the physical world we are indeed god-forsaken as regards thought. 'Thus the outer glory, the edifice of our civilization, will collapse all of a sudden; present forms of life will vanish without trace' (29.1.11), like all previous cultures.

To ask in the name of Christ is to do so as effective agent of his will ('keep my commandments'), not to ask for what you personally want, invoking his name. The commandment of Christ is love, especially within an esoteric relationship, when profound secrets are already passed at the first stage of 'study' appropriate to today. To ask of Christ we must learn his language, in which we hear of Earth evolution. Then he will stand by us and answer as a brother. The Christ stream will lead by way of brotherly feeling and insight to morality.

The great teachers have never taught an absolute truth, but what is right for humanity at that time. We may think of the gradual descent of the Cosmic Intelligence of Michael between Golgotha and the fifteenth century, centred on the ninth. The certainty first experienced in mathematics, which then became widespread, must be extended to the whole of spiritual and social life (Gal. 5:16–24). Wisdom is a single whole, and will be the means of creating the great brotherhood of humanity. On this depends the development from 'I am with you' (v. 9) to 'I in you' (v. 20).

The promise to show himself to ones who love him (v. 21) becomes real in our present age through the Appearing (*epiphaneia*), the first of the three stages of the Second Coming: 'the appearing of him who dwells in unapproachable light whom no man has ever seen or can see' (1 Tim. 6:14–16). Only one who like the disciples (v. 17) has become a 'son of man' (i.e. has developed the consciousness soul) sees him as etheric phenomenon in the soul world. This is today being reported, and will increase. But beware false prophets (Mark 13:21–3).

14:22–31 *My Peace I Give to You*

22 Judas (not Iscariot) says, Lord, what has happened that you are about to show yourself to us, and not to the world? **23** Jesus replied, If anyone loves me he will keep my word, and my Father will love him, and we will come to him and make abode with him. **24** He who does not love me does not keep my words; and the word which you hear is not mine, but that of the Father who sent me. **25** I have spoken of these things to you while abiding with you; **26** but the Counsellor, the Holy Spirit, whom the Father will send in my name, will teach you all things and remind you of all that 'I' told you.

27 Peace I leave to you, my peace I give to you; not as the world gives do 'I' give to you. Let not your heart be troubled, nor let it be fearful. **28** You heard that 'I' told you, I go, and come to you. If you loved me, you would have rejoiced that I go to the Father, because the Father is greater than I. **29** And now I have told you before it happens, so that when it happens you may have trust. **30** I will no longer speak many things with you, for the ruler of the world is coming; and he has nothing in me. **31** But I act so that the world may know that I love the Father, and do as the Father commanded me. Rise, let us go hence.

Judas, the phlegmatic, must be Thaddeus (Mark 3:18) son of James (Luke 6:16). He expected a Messiah for all Jews, and is upset by sensing polarization between the close disciples and others. He is advised to augment love (vv. 23,24) with trust(v. 29).

The Counsellor is now revealed as the Holy Spirit, an activity of the Trinity or Cosmic Ego, as thinking is an activity of our ego. If work with the Spirit of Truth has become wholly free of personal wishes, it descends into the purified or virgin soul with spiritual light and creative impulses for the future. The part of the astral body comprising right, beautiful and virtuous relationships, thus transformed by the 'I' to Spirit Self, is called in Christian esotericism the Holy Spirit.

'The Holy Spirit, the ruler of Ancient Moon with its wisdom, had been displaced at the Fall by Lucifer, the unholy spirit and sponsor of intellectuality and art. But at Golgotha (Luke 23:42) the transforming of Lucifer to Holy Spirit begins (p. 126), through whom human beings may retain their 'I'-consciousness and Christ still live within them' (22.3.09). The Spirit was first given in the inner room by Christ (20:22, recognized only by John) and openly by the Father at Pentecost (Acts 2:2) to the disciples and those who feel Christ as 'I in you', enabling them to grasp the spirit in freedom. Had Christ not gone he would be followed instinctively, and there could be no freedom.

The Holy Spirit, which underlies all perception and consciousness of the spiritual, is also the healing spirit — one who unites with it receives the power of healing.

The only means of bringing about universal brotherhood is the worldwide spread of esoteric knowledge. True peace is not mere order and harmony, but a gift of Christ to the Spirit Self. His peace is in fact the soul of a new world order. Then a common understanding in the spiritual-religious-social sphere will form in human souls a new sheath around the earth (p. 131).

The casting out of the 'ruler of this world' has already been assured (12:31); but it is a long process, as John's Book of Revelation makes clear. However, it is in our present fifth age with the imminent incarnation of Ahriman that the struggle against the Antichrist begins. 'Ahriman will set up an esoteric school in which spiritual experience can be gained without the necessary effort, but everyone will have different experiences, which will lead to chaos' (15.11.19).

The final call is usually regarded as the end of the original discourse, which John forgot to delete when expanding it. But it is a call for a rise in consciousness — lift up your hearts and minds — in preparation for what follows. 'Us', the lower ego, must go to meet the adversary, before the spirit can enter as Spirit Self.

15:1–8 'I' Am the True Vine[*]

1 'I' am the true vine, and my Father is the vine-dresser. 2 Every branch in me not bearing fruit he removes, and every one that bears fruit he prunes to bear more fruit. 3 You are now clean because of the word that I have spoken to you: 4 abide in me, and 'I' in you. As the branch cannot bear fruit from itself unless it remains on the vine, neither can you unless you abide in me. 5 'I' am the vine, you the branches. He who abides in me and 'I' in him bears much fruit, for apart from me you can do nothing. 6 Unless anyone abides in me, he is cast out like the branch and withers, and they gather them up and throw them into the fire,

---

[*]Seventh stage of development of the 'I am' (the true ego).

and they are burned. **7** If you abide in me and my words abide in you, ask whatever you wish and it shall happen to you. **8** By this is my Father glorified, that you bear much fruit and will be disciples of mine.

This chapter describes the conflict in the sixth age (Philadel-phia – Rev. 3:7) between those who follow Jesus Christ inly and 'the world', including those who are indifferent and pursue their material aims. This age will start in AD 3573.

The last of the seven great 'I am' sayings is the metamorphosis of a terminology of the Essenes, who called one who extended his memory to previous generations a 'living branch', whereas one who shrank within a single personality was called a 'severed branch'. That looked backward to the old group soul, and the Baptist condemned it (Luke 3:7-9). But here the image looks forward to the new community in Christ, where even that which bears good fruit is to be 'pruned' (here it means disposal of the lower ego).

The imagination teaches that 'in place of group soul or race, humanity will be divided in future into the good and the evil races' (24.6.08), those who bear fruit or those who are thrown into the fire and burned. The sixth age is a metamorphosis of the second (Persian) age when Zarathustra preached the polarity between Ahura Mazda, the sun god, and Ahriman, the power of darkness. Christ's specific gift for this age is Seership.

'Bearing fruit' and 'abide in me' are both said five times, pointing to the sphere of practical earthly work. Each 'I' should say: I am one of the pruned branches; then it will have the spirit of the good community within it. Christ here provides the spiritual lifeblood for all existing races. And then the Father, the spirit of common origin, may, when love between blood brothers vanishes, enter the individual 'I' for it to build its own abode within the universal brotherhood of Spirit Self.

15:9-17 The Command of Love

9 As the Father loved me, I also loved you. Abide in my love. **10** If you keep my commandments you will abide in my love, as 'I' have kept the commandments of my Father and abide in his love. **11** I have said these things to you that my joy may be in you, and your joy may be full. **12** This is my commandment, that you love one another as I loved you. **13** Greater love has no man than this, that he should lay down his soul for his friends. **14** You are my friends if you do what 'I' command you. **15** I no longer call you servants, because the servant does not know what his master is doing; but I have called you friends, because I made known to you all that I heard from my Father. **16** You did not choose me, but 'I' chose you, and appointed you to go and to bear fruit, and your fruit should abide, that whatever you may ask the Father in my name, he may give you. **17** This I command you, that you love one another.

The command of love was first given at 13:34, enhanced to 'as I loved you'. It recurred in 14:15,21-4,31 in the context of the love between Father, Son and the 'I'. Now it is spiritualized as an absolute and continuing imperative for the good race: abide in my love by keeping my commandment. Only slowly is the etheric body, the body of love, changed into Life Spirit through the truths of anthroposophy. The shining of Life Spirit from above into Spirit Self is the Christian concept of Grace. It will be especially important at the end of the sixth age. Future joy will depend on this (v. 11).

The greatest love will be to lay down one's *psyche* for one's friends (10:11-18). This is normally translated 'to lay down one's life', which may be necessary. But for the Greeks, for whom this Gospel was written, *psyche* was the normal word for soul. Moreover, 'if we have gravely harmed someone, we may when reincarnating feel the need freely to give them our more perfect soul, and take for ourselves that which we damaged. Without such future deeds, Earth evolution will be unable to reach its goal. This is part of the Mysteries of the Father' (19.11.22): 'as the Father loved me' (v. 9).

So long as any spiritual impulse remains unconscious we are slaves; hence the step from 'disciple' to 'friend' depends on developing higher consciousness as a 'son of God', but also on being chosen. Whereas the Jews felt themselves to be a chosen race, Christians are individually chosen (v. 16) according to their karma. It is the 'making known of the Father' that enables us to act out of full knowledge in freedom as a 'friend' of Christ.

15:18–27 Hatred and Sin

18 If the world hates you, Know that it has hated me before you. **19** If you were of the world, the world would have cared for its own; but because you are not of the world, but 'I' chose you out of the world, therefore the world hates you. **20** Remember the words 'I' said to you: a servant is not greater than his master. If they persecuted me, they will also persecute you; if they kept my word, they will also keep yours. **21** But they will do all this to you on account of my name, because they do not know the one who sent me. **22** If I had not come and spoken to them they would not have sin; but now they have no excuse for their sin. **23** One who hates me also hates my Father. **24** If I had not done among them deeds such as no one else did, they would not have sin; but now they have both seen and hated both me and my Father. **25** But it fulfils the word written in their law, They hated me freely. **26** When the Counsellor comes whom 'I' will send to you from the Father, namely the Spirit of Truth which proceeds from the Father, He will testify concerning me; **27** and you too are witnesses, because you are with me from the start.

The Jews already hated Jesus because he revealed their deeds as evil (7:7). Hatred is an expression of the ahrimanic powers that must be overcome in the sixth age. Their sin was that they saw Christ's deeds yet rejected him (9:41). But because his deeds were those of the Father, they are also hating the Father (v. 23). The plain fact is that Christians will in future ages have to undergo the suffering already undergone by Christ, which will result, more than anything else could, in their inner strengthening.

But the crisis of the sixth age will be of a different order: 'It is just with God to repay with affliction those afflicting you ... at the Revelation (*apokalypsis*) of the Lord Jesus from heaven with his angels of power in flaming fire, inflicting full vengeance on those who do not know God ... who will pay the penalty of eternal destruction from the face of the Lord ...' (2 Thess. 1:6–9). This is the time of Christ (2:4). 'Feeling now predominates, enabling the soul to enter lower spiritland, where Christ will reveal himself in sound, and from his astral body of light fill receptive souls with the Word' (18.11.11).

Starting around the end of the sixth age, reproduction as we know it will gradually cease, physical bodies being then created through the larynx. 'The Lost Word of unisexual conception is thus found again, but as a fiery male capacity, whilst females take the lead in the spiritual life' (the opposite of primeval times) (23.10.05). Some individuals will become selfless again as sexuality drops away. And for those like the disciples who receive the Holy Spirit in the form of Spirit Self, the Spirit of Truth who speaks in them (14:17) will testify to Christ. 'Spirit of Truth' means the new ability to find the truth out of oneself, independent of all sense perception. He speaks in the 'I am' form. 'Blessed are the peacemakers (they who draw down the Spirit Self) for they shall be called the children of God' (Matt. 5:9).

16:1–11 The War of All Against All

1 I have said these things to you so that you are not falling away. **2** They will exclude you from the synagogue; but a time comes when whoever kills you thinks to offer service to God. **3** And they will do this because they Knew neither the Father nor me. **4** But I have said this to you so that, when their time comes, you may remember that 'I' told you. I did not say this to you from the start because I was with you. **5** But now I go to the One who sent me, and not one of you questions, Where are you going? **6** But because I have said this to you, sorrow has filled your hearts. **7** But 'I' tell you the truth, it is better for you that 'I' should go away. For if I do not go away, the Counsellor will not come to you; but if I go, I will send him to you. **8** And when he comes he will convince the world of sin, of rectitude, and of judgement: **9** of sin, because they do not believe in me; **10** of rectitude, because

I am going to the Father and you will no longer see me; **11** of judgement, because the ruler of this world has been judged.

This chapter foresees the seventh age (from 5735 to about AD 7900) and the end of the post-Atlantean epoch. In this age, morality is predominant; whereas immorality will paralyse the soul. The false concept of killing under the delusion of serving God has already a long history, from martyrdom to the Inquisition. Today it is a motivation for terrorism. But this is only a foretaste of the war of all against all, which for the majority who have not become penetrated by the Christ-principle in the right way will usurp the place of love. 'Blessed are they that are persecuted for righteousness' sake, for theirs is the kingdom of heaven' (Matt. 5:10). That will bring the whole post-Atlantean epoch to an end.

Christ's power was such that 'if he had remained physically, his power would overwhelm human bodies, as it did even that of Jesus in three years' (1.4.07). People would not prepare to be deified creators, and the earth would go back to the Father. The desire-imbued ego must be renounced (the word *ego* is withheld between vv. 7 and 26) in order for the Holy Spirit to replace it as Spirit Self. The whole post-Atlantean epoch will end in devastating moral entanglements based on egoism.

The text of verses 8 to 11 is obscure. The judicial terminology suggests that the good and evil streams are now separate. Disbelief is in opposition to the divine 'I' that is the crux of Christianity (8:24). Rectitude, uprightness, is the outpouring of brotherly love through the 'I' in the sentient soul, the basic quality of the 'I'. And correct judgement of 'the ruler of this world' is the essential task of the 'I' in the intellectual soul. All three thus point to 'the battle against the asuric powers that directly attack the "I"', especially in the seventh age' (8.2.10).

16:12–22 Grief Will Turn to Joy

12 I have still many things to tell you, but you cannot bear them now. **13** But when He, the Spirit of Truth comes, he will guide you into all the truth; for he will not speak from himself, but he will speak what he will hear, and will proclaim to you the things to come. **14** He will glorify me, because he will receive and declare to you that which is mine. **15** All that the Father has is mine; that is why I said that he receives and will proclaim to you of that which is mine. **16** A short time, and you will no longer see me; and again a short time and you will behold me. **17** So some of his disciples said to one another, What is this that he tells us: a short time and you will not see me, and again a short time and you will behold me [and, because I am going to the Father]? **18** So they said, What is this [which he says], the 'short time'? We do not know what he means. **19** Jesus understood that they wanted to question him, and said, Are you asking one another about this because I said, A short time and you do not see me, and again a short time and you will behold me? **20** Truly I tell[s] you that you will weep and lament, and the world will rejoice; you will be grieved, but your grief will turn to joy. **21** When a woman gives birth she has grief, because her hour came; but when she brings forth the child she no longer remembers the anguish, because of the joy that a man was born into the world. **22** So you indeed now have grief; but I will behold you again, and your heart will rejoice, and no one will take your joy from you.

Whilst the Gospels are wholly true (when errors of copyists and translators are surmounted), they are not the whole truth. Not only did Christ continue to teach between the Resurrection and the Ascension for 40 days (Acts 1:3). His revelation in accord with the Spirit of Truth (v. 13) is a continuing one until the end of the earth, and without necessarily direct vision of the mysteries.

The sevenfold repetition of 'a short time' reads today as almost ridiculous. It is usually interpreted as the hours between crucifixion and bodily resurrection. But a life is a 'short time' compared to the period from death to rebirth; and seven lives reach on average to the end of the post-Atlantean epoch. This is also a reminder that the seventh age (Laodicea — Rev. 3:14) is a metamorphosis of the first (Indian) age, when teaching was based on rhythmic repetition, as children get tables 'by heart'.

The clear distinction between 'see' and 'behold' (v. 16) invites the comparison of Jesus' death and resurrection with the process of initiation; but the disciples (and modern theologians) do not recognize this because Judaism had no recent tradition of initiation, only of prophecy. In the seventh age the gift of prophecy (v. 13) will become widespread as a gift of Christ.

'A man was born' (v. 21) — rather than 'a child' — suggests, in the context of birth through the larynx, that it will be possible for Christ to manifest at the Second Presence (*parousia,* not *erchetai* — Matt. 24) 'in higher spiritland in his true Ego of inconceivable sublimity as Earth Spirit' (18.11.11). 'We who are alive shall be caught up in the clouds ... to meet the Lord in the air ...' (1 Thess. 4:17). A small group of people who have taken the spiritual principle into themselves will be saved from the general destruction. We might expect (v. 22) that 'you will behold me again', but in the spirit, 'to be beheld' by a spiritual being is the real experience.

16:23–33 I Have Overcome the World

23 In that day you will not request anything of me. Truly I tell[s] you, whatever you ask the Father he will give you in my name. **24** Until now you did not ask anything in my name; ask and you will receive, that your joy may be full. **25** I have said these things to you in allegories; a time comes when I will no longer speak to you in allegories, but will declare to you plainly about the Father. **26** In that day you will ask in my name, and I do not tell you that 'I' will request the Father concerning you; **27** for the Father himself loves you because you have loved me, and have believed that 'I' came from God. **28** I [came out of the Father and] have come into the world. I leave the world again and go to the Father. **29** His disciples say, Look, now you speak plainly, not in allegory. **30** Now we know that you know all, and have no need for anyone to question you; by this we believe that you came from God. **31** Jesus answered, Do you now believe [?]. **32** Behold, a time comes, and has come, when you are each dispersed to your own, and leave me alone; and I am not alone, because the Father is with me. **33** I have said these things to you, that in me you may have peace. You [will] have anguish in the world; but cheer up, 'I' have overcome the world.

The discourse concludes in a mood of hope, which builds up the physical body for a new life. Previously (14:14) the disciples were told 'if you ask me anything in my name'. But now they are to 'ask the Father in my name'. For the disciples direct approach through Intuition to the Father becomes possible because he loves them (*philein,* p. 141). 'To the extent that a person has that which ennobles and transforms the physical body, so far has he the Father within him' (25.3.07). They experience in advance what will be possible when Christ is again present.

The disciples suddenly realized that both the most significant feature and the greatest illusion of the world around them is the outer expression of the Father, that death is the name of the ever-living Father, though today distorted by Lucifer and Ahriman. They now understood that Christ came forth from death in its true form, from the Life Father, and that he is going to his death. He thereby overcomes death for the future of the world, to be replaced by metamorphosis in the sixth main epoch (seals — Rev. 6). 'The new Sun of Life would never rise, had not death entered the world and been overcome by Christ. He came to create a true image and form of the living Father God. From this, mankind may come to understand what follows, and obtain nourishment for all time to come' (6.7.09).

At the end of this long discourse, which concludes in a mood of positivity, the disciples are 'on their own' as individuals, at peace in themselves with the final word of hope, the quality which must be developed in physical existence in this final age of the post-Atlantean condition of life.

The Divine Prayer

The prayer of one member of the Trinity to another! Who but one initiated by Christ himself dare (in those days) write down such a thing?

Rudolf Steiner withholds comment on this chapter in his lectures. But he advised its inclusion in the Last Anointment service of the Christian Community.

17:1–5 His Prayer for His Ordeal

1 Jesus said these things, and lifting up his eyes to heaven said, Father, the time has come; glorify thy Son, that the Son may glorify thee, **2** as thou gavest him authority over all flesh, that to all that thou hast given him he may give eternal life. [**3** And this is eternal life, that they may know thee, the only true God, and Jesus Christ whom thou didst send.] **4** 'I' glorified thee on earth, finishing the work which thou hast given me that I should do; **5** and now, glorify thou me, Father, with thyself, with the glory which I had, to be with thee before the world was.

17:6–19 His Prayer for the Apostles

6 I revealed thy name to the men whom thou gavest to me out of the world. Thine they were, and to me thou gavest them, and they have kept thy word. **7** Now they know that everything thou hast given to me is from thee; **8** for the words thou gavest me I gave to them, and they received them and Knew truly that I came forth from thee, and they believed that thou didst send me. **9** 'I' pray for them; I do not pray for the world, but for those whom thou hast given me, because they are thine, **10** and all that are mine are thine, and thine mine, and I have been glorified in them. **11** I am no longer in the world, and they are in the world, and I come to thee. Holy Father, keep in thy name those whom thou hast given to me, that they be one as we are. **12** When I was with them, 'I' kept in thy name those whom thou hast given to me, and I guarded them, and not one of them perished except the son of perdition, that the scripture might be fulfilled. **13** But now I come to thee, and I speak these things in the world that they may have my joy fulfilled in themselves. **14** 'I' have given them thy word, and the world hated them because they are not of the world, [as 'I' am not of the world]. **15** I do not pray that thou shouldst take them out of the world, but that thou shouldst keep them from evil. **16** They are not of the world, as 'I' am not of the world. **17** Sanctify them in the truth; thy word is truth. **18** As thou didst send me into the world, I also sent them into the world; **19** and on their behalf 'I' sanctify myself, that they also may be sanctified in truth.

17:20–6 His Prayer for All Committed Through Their Word

20 I do not however pray only for these, but also for those believing me inly through their word, **21** that all may be one as thou, Father, in me and I in thee, that they may also be in us, that the world may believe that thou didst send me. **22** And I have given to them the glory which thou hast given to me, that they may be one as we are one; **23** 'I' in them and thou in me, that they may be perfected into one, that the world may know that thou didst send me, and didst love them as thou didst love me. **24** Father, I wish that where 'I' am, those also whom thou hast given to me may be with me, that they may behold my glory which thou hast given to me because thou didst love me before the foundation of the world. **25** Righteous Father, the world indeed Knew thee not, but 'I' Knew thee, and these Knew that thou didst send me; **26** and I made Known to them and will make Known thy name, that the love with which thou didst love me may be in them, and I in them.

The Arraignment

18:1–12 The Arrest

1 Having said these things, Jesus went out with his disciples across the Kidron wadi, where there was a garden which he and his disciples entered. **2** Now Judas, who was betraying him, also knew the place, because Jesus often met there with his disciples. **3** So Judas, taking the cohort and attendants from the chief priests and Pharisees, comes there with lanterns and torches and weapons. **4** Jesus, knowing all that was coming to him, stood forth and says to them, Whom do you seek? **5** They answered, Jesus of Nazareth. He tells them, 'I' am. Now Judas, betraying him, also stood with them. **6** So when he told them, 'I' am, they backed away and fell to the ground. **7** So again he asked them, Whom do you seek? And they said, Jesus of Nazareth. **8** Jesus answered, I told you that 'I' am; so if you seek me, allow these to go; **9** that the word which he had spoken might be fulfilled; Of those whom thou gavest me, I lost not one. **10** So Simon Peter, having a short sword, drew it and smote the high priest's servant and cut off his right ear; the servant's name was Malchus. **11** So Jesus said to Peter, Sheathe the sword; the cup which the Father has given me, shall I not drink it? **12** So the cohort and their captain and the attendants of the Jews took Jesus and bound him.

Mark (14:26) says 'when they had sung a hymn they went out'. The Acts of John (94/5)[*] elaborates: 'He bade us therefore make as it were a ring, holding one another's hands, and himself standing in the middle he said, 'Answer Amen to me.' He began then to sing a hymn, saying, 'Glory to thee, Father,' and we, going about in a circle answered him, 'Amen.' 'Glory to thee,

---

[*] A Manichaean work of the mid-second century. See M.R. James, *The Apocryphal New Testament*, Oxford 1924.

Word.' 'Amen' (and so on for 30 lines). 'Now answer to my dancing. Behold thyself in me who speaks; and seeing what I do, keep silent about my mysteries. For this Passion of Manhood, which I am about to suffer, is thine ...'

John omits 'the agony in the garden' of Gethsemane described by Mark 14:32–42. Three times Jesus prayed 'not as I will, but as thou wilt' (cf. 12:27), 'and his sweat became as great drops of blood falling to the earth'. Only Peter, James and John could be led to experience this in spiritual (not merely astral) vision – they heard as well as saw – but each time they fell back into a dream state. Hence they did not defend Jesus.

Mark adds (14:51f.) that during the arrest 'a certain young man followed him, clothed in a *sindon* over his naked body, and they seize him; and he, leaving the *sindon*, fled naked'. 'This is an imagination of the separation of the youthful cosmic element of Christ himself from the body of Jesus, the Son of Man, who suffered death alone' (23.9.12). (Full mystic experience of such loneliness is to be aware of a share in the guilt of slaying the Divinity.) It is the entirely naked new cosmic impulse, which united with the earth, and transforms human moral concepts into the seed-force for cosmic evolution. But such a deed requires a physical correlate, and it also sounds like the young man in a *sindon* (p. 82) who was 'told what to do', Lazarus/John himself. He quickly returns to accompany Jesus (v. 15). Christ however remained united with the *soul* of Jesus, so that the pains of physical injury and death could become known in the realm of the Gods. He now guides the body entirely from outside, as will progressive humanity in the sixth main epoch.

John makes clear that Jesus retained control and stood forth. 'Or do you think that I cannot ask my Father to send me more than twelve legions of Angels?' (Matt. 26:53). This was a tremendous deed of renunciation, more powerful in spirit than any strengthening of the will. It made the kiss of Judas superfluous (Mark 14:44–5). Jesus also inaugurated the dispersal of the disciples (v. 8) – Mark 14:50 says they fled in fear.

That the Jews brought a Roman cohort (600 men, clearly only a detachment) shows that they feared an insurrection. It would be the Jewish attendants who fell back, hearing 'I am', the name of their God. The choleric Peter cut off the symbolic ear of Inspiration. Malchus is to become *Malchut*, the 'kingdom' of the senses, where the ego is fully conscious. But Luke 22:50 adds that Jesus healed the wound.

18:13–27 *Before the High Priests. The Denial*

13 First they led him to Annas; for he was father-in-law to Caiaphas, high priest that year; **14** it was Caiaphas who had advised the Jews that it was better for one man to die on behalf of the people. **15** Simon Peter and another disciple followed Jesus; and that disciple was Known to the high priest, and went in with Jesus into the court of the high priest, **16** while Peter stood outside at the door. The other disciple Known to the high priest therefore went out and told the portress, and brought Peter in. **17** So the maid, the portress, says to Peter, Are you not also one of this man's disciples? He says, I am not. **18** The servants and attendants, having made a fire because it was cold, were warming themselves; and Peter was also standing with them, warming himself.

19 The high priest questioned Jesus about his disciples and about his teaching. **20** Jesus answered, 'I' have spoken plainly to the world; 'I' always taught in synagogue and in the temple, where all Jews come together, and I spoke nothing in secret. **21** Why do you question me? Ask those who heard what I spoke to them; look, they know what 'I' said. **22** As he said this, one of the attendants standing by gave Jesus a slap, saying, Is that how you answer the high priest? **23** Jesus answered, If I spoke ill, testify to the evil, but if well, why do you hit me? **24** So Annas sent him bound to Caiaphas the high priest.

25 Now Simon Peter was standing and warming himself. So they said to him, are you not also one of his disciples? He denied and said, I am not. **26** One of the servants of the high priest, a relative of him whose ear Peter cut off, says, Did 'I' not see you in the garden with him? **27** So again Peter denied; and at once a cock crowed.

Annas was a previous high priest, deposed 15 years before, but revered by the Jews accordingly. We do not know of a disciple other than Lazarus/John likely to be known to Annas – the others were from Galilee. But as a well-educated 'rich young man' (p. 82) he may well have been.

The direct questioning was illegal. Jesus had of course spoken to the Twelve in secret (e.g. 6:3, Mark 4:34). He did not speak publicly without a parable, but explained everything privately to his disciples. But he had no other secret following. His reply can be seen as a request for witnesses; and the slap in response was also illegal. This pre-trial may be a holding move until Caiaphas was ready. The trial before the latter described by the synoptics included false witnesses (Mark 14:56), the formal accusation of blasphemy, and the necessary decision of the Sanhedrin. John may have recalled the latter as decided in advance (11:53). There are other inconsistencies of detail between John (an initiate and participant) and the synoptics (clairvoyants working with tradition).

Peter, the senior of the Twelve, has been having a difficult time lately (13:10, 13:28, 18:11) and now comes his threefold denial. 'This was because his normal consciousness had been replaced since the Transfiguration by a kind of dreamlike higher consciousness, in which he had spiritual experiences' (2.10.13). At least he did not abandon Jesus at once.

18:28–38 Before Pilate

28 So they lead Jesus from Caiaphas to the praetorium; it was early; and they did not enter the praetoruim, lest they be defiled, but might eat the Passover. **29** So Pilate went outside to them and says, What accusation do you bring against this man? **30** They replied, Unless this fellow was doing evil, we would not have delivered him to you. **31** Pilate said, Take him yourselves, and judge him according to your law. The Jews said, It is not lawful for us to kill anyone; **32** that might be fulfilled the word which Jesus said, signifying by what death he was about to die.

33 So Pilate re-entered the praetorium, and calling Jesus said, You are the King of the Jews? **34** Jesus: Do you say this from yourself, or have others told you about me? **35** Pilate: Am 'I' a Jew? Your nation and the chief priests delivered you to me; what did you do? **36** Jesus: My kingdom is not of this world; if my kingdom were of this world, my attendants would have fought, that I should not have been delivered to the Jews; but now my kingdom is not from there. **37** Pilate: Are you not really a king? Jesus: You say that I am a king. 'I' have been born for this, and for this I have come into the world, that I might testify to the truth; everyone who is of the truth hears my voice. **38** Pilate: What is truth?

Pontius Pilate, the Roman procurator of Judea AD 26–36, showed weakness from the start by going out to the Jews before any formal charge had been made. They could have washed away any formal defilement by a bath before sunset.

'According to the Akashic Record the answer to Pilate's question was, "This, you alone may give as answer," namely no one may ever give such an answer in reference to himself.' (8.10.11). The explanation by Jesus meant that his kingdom which was 'not of this world' should draw increasingly into that part of every individual that is also 'not of this world' (whereas Jesuits require submission to 'king Jesus' in this world). Pilate is at first sympathetic, accepting as harmless that Jesus be called a king (6:15, 12:13).

John could only know of the conversation by clairaudience. Pilate's further question 'What is truth?' can now be approached through 14:17, the Spirit of Truth or Counsellor, the Holy Spirit, and involves the unsheathing of the Spirit Self.

18:38–19:6 Scourging and Crown of Thorns

Having said this, he went out again to the Jews, and tells them, 'I' find no crime in him. **39** But you have a custom that I should release one to you at the Passover; will you therefore have me release to you the king of the Jews? **40** They cried out again, Not this fellow, but Barabbas. But Barabbas was a bandit.

19:1 So then Pilate took Jesus and scourged him. **2** The soldiers plaited a crown of thorns and put it on his head, and threw around him a crimson robe, **3** and came up to him and said, Hail, king of the Jews; and they slapped him. **4** Pilate again went outside and says, Look, I bring him out to you, that you may know that I find no crime in him. **5** So Jesus came out, wearing the thorny wreath and the crimson robe. And he says to them, Behold the Man! **6** When the chief priests and attendants saw him, they shouted, Crucify, crucify! Pilate says, You take and crucify him, for 'I' find no crime in him.

No custom of release at Passover is known outside the Gospels. Barabbas was imprisoned for insurrection and murder (Luke 23:19). But it is ironic that 'Barabbas' means 'son of the father', and ancient authorities even call him Jesus Barabbas (Matt. 27:16 mg.). So he may stand for the Double of Jesus. 'Jesus had no karma of his own; he suffered without reason' (3.10.13). Luke (23:6–12) reports that Pilate sent Jesus to Herod, who questioned him without reply, so Herod's soldiers also mocked and arrayed him before sending him back to Pilate.

Scourging was illegal without a Roman trial. Pilate represents the Roman intellect, which still scourges mankind. Scourging represents the second stage of the Christian ego-initiation for the fourth (mind-soul) age, which the great mystics experienced. It began with the feeling that people to whom one gives of one's best will not acknowledge it, represented by the slap. Then one pictures for months that all possible pain and suffering, hardships and hindrances, troubles and sorrows come upon one, and how one stands erect through all the adversity, defending what one finds holy. One has a wider sense of life, and love for all beings. This is called 'the way to the Father'. At length one feels oneself beaten from all sides, a stinging, pricking or itching sensation all over the body. And one has an astral vision of oneself being scourged in Christ (List α). For the present age of the spiritual soul this is replaced by Imaginative knowledge, which 'sees' the etheric and astral bodies imaginatively in terms

of the senses. The ideal of becoming as chaste as the plant cap-
tivates heart, mind and soul; above the seed a small flame
appears, every stone speaks of the indwelling Earth Spirit. It is a
matter of relating to the world in moral terms. This works via the
individual etheric body and the blood to heal and reform the
organism. European pupils should take their time over this
stage—it is easy to damage one's progress (List β).

Philo records a similar mock enthronement at Alexandria; the
crown was probably spiky palm leaves arranged as sun rays, and
the robe blood-red. Mocking, too, should only occur after a
verdict. ('Behold the Man' was foretold—Zech. 6:12.)

At the third stage of the Christian mind-soul initiation, the
pupil imagined for months that his highest 'I', his holiest possession, was subjected to jeers and jibes, scorn and derision; he
must accept it without anger, calmly, firmly, ready to stand alone
although despised as worthless. Then the forebrain sensed genuine pain, and the 'crown of thorns' was experienced in astral
vision. The double appears, thinking feeling and willing separate
as monsters that must be controlled (p. 54). Then Christ appears,
looking down on the suffering overcome, and leads the pupil
beyond the earthly to the cosmic (List α). On the modern
Christian-Rosicrucian path this is replaced by the exercises for
Inspiration, learning to read the occult script, which expresses
the harmony of the spheres. All drives and instincts are purified,
the world soul is perceived, and the imagination of the Holy
Grail arises. The spiritual reality as inner word floats above all
things as pictures or lines of force. This brings about a genuine
intercourse with the Beings of the Hierarchies. Spiritual science
will become increasingly subject to such mockery before it is
fully established (List β).

19:7–16 Pilate's Judgement

7 The Jews answered, We have a law, and according to the law he
ought to die because he made himself Son of God. 8 When Pilate
heard this word he was very afraid, 9 and entered the praetoruim
again, and says to Jesus, Where are you from? But Jesus did not
answer. 10 So Pilate says, Do you not speak to me? Do you not

know that I have authority to release you and I have authority to crucify you? **11** Jesus answered, You would have no authority over me unless it had been given you from above; therefore he who delivered me to you has greater sin. **12** From this Pilate sought to release him; but the Jews shouted, If you release this fellow you are no friend of Caesar; everyone making himself a king speaks against Caesar. **13** So Pilate, hearing this, brought Jesus outside, and sat on a judgement seat at a place called Pavement (in Hebrew, Gabbatha). **14** Now it was about midday on the eve of the Passover. He says to the Jews, Behold your King. **15** So they shouted, Take him, take him, crucify him! Pilate says to them, Shall I crucify your king? The chief priests replied, We have no king but Caesar. **16** So then he delivered him to [satisfy] them, that he should be crucified.

Jesus is standing between the hatred of the Jews and the fear and arrogance of Pilate, who was afraid that an insurrection might damage his reputation as procurator. And what if it were the Son of God before him? He is reminded of his wife's dream not to get involved (Matt. 27:19). So he turns again to question Jesus, whose body has become too sick and feeble to answer a pointless question. When he tries to assert his authority, Jesus relieves him of ultimate responsibility (v. 11). He therefore tries publicly to wash his hands of the matter (Matt. 27:24); but the contact with water actually increases his sensitivity. The moral struggle of Pilate must in due course be felt by every individual.

It is now midday (v. 14), the Passover lambs were slaughtered in the temple between 3 and 6 p.m. The Pavement, emphasized by its Hebrew name, is the hard rock bottom of the mineral element of Earth evolution, from which the whole destiny of the Earth can only be reflected in a new direction upwards. The Jews are so desperate that they invoke the name of Caesar, whom Romans were to regard as himself a god. By claiming that he was their only king, they not only commit perjury but also blasphemy, for according to their scripture (which they so readily quote when it suits them) God was their king (Judg. 8:23). 'They show that they have no knowledge of what the human being is — humanity has lost itself' (12.7.14).

The Jewish practice was to stone to death (8:59) but they call for crucifixion, which only Roman soldiers were allowed to perform. Not only do they hope to evade responsibility, but Jesus himself would in their view be under curse (Deut. 21:22, cf. Gal. 3:13).

Golgotha*

19:17–24 The Crucifixion

17 So they took Jesus, and he went out carrying the cross-beam for himself to what was called the Place of a Skull (in Hebrew, Golgotha). **18** There they crucified him, and with him two others on this side and that; and Jesus in the middle. **19** Pilate also wrote a title and put it on the cross; on it was written, 'Jesus of Nazareth, the King of the Jews'. **20** Many of the Jews accordingly read this title, because the place where Jesus was crucified was near the city, and it was written in Hebrew, Latin and Greek. **21** The chief priests of the Jews said to Pilate, Do not write 'the King of the Jews' but that 'He said, I am King of the Jews'. **22** Pilate replied, What I have written I have written.

23 When the soldiers crucified Jesus they took his clothes and made four parts, a part for each soldier, and the tunic. Now the tunic was seamless, woven throughout from the top. **24** So they said to one another, Let us not tear it, but let us cast lots for it, whose it shall be; that the scripture might be fulfilled: They parted my garments among them, and for my raiment they cast a lot. So these things the soldiers did.

All the sufferings and agonies of Christ, all the mockery and scorn, the contempt and shame, were infinitely harder for him than for a human being. The synoptics add the help given by Simon of Cyrene (Mark 15:21).

In many ancient mysteries the candidate had been bound for a time with hands outstretched in the form of a cross. This originally signified the plant (descending to earth), the animal (horizontal) and the human being (directed to the sun). But the Romans transformed it to an instrument of death. The three crosses signify balance between blood relationship and self-seeking.

---

*The remaining sections draw heavily from *The Mystery of the Resurrection* by Sergei O. Prokofieff, Temple Lodge, Forest Row 2010.

'The Temple Legend tells that the wood of the cross was once a bridge between the lower nature and the spirit. But this wood died, and became the law. Then Jesus took the cross on his shoulders, uniting the world's problems with his conscience, which gave it new life. When a human being becomes able to carry the cross like an instrument, making the law his own, he can reunite the two natures and act in freedom and love' (29.5.05).

Only Luke (23:42) mentions that while one of the criminals (representing Ahriman) hurled insults at Jesus, the other (representing Lucifer) recognized his innocence, and was told: Today you will be with me in Paradise. This hints at the fact that 'the Holy Spirit (not yet given) is none other than the unholy spirit, Lucifer, gradually resurrected by Christ in higher, purer glory as the spirit of independent understanding, interwoven with wisdom. Lucifer is the "light-bearer", Christ *is* the light. When an individual gains insight into what Christ truly is, he redeems both himself and the associated luciferic beings' (22.3.09). The Holy Spirit is thus reborn from the destruction, the pain, endured on the cross.

The title INRI (v. 19), in Hebrew *Jam Nur Ruach Jabascha*, also means water, fire, air, rock. The whole power of these elements is renewed by Christ as he becomes Spirit of the Earth. People have divided up the earth (v. 23), but the air — the tunic woven 'from above' — from which the breath of life was poured into mankind with the first rudiments of the ego (Gen. 2:7), cannot be divided. It is the outer symbol for the love hovering about the globe, which will later unite mankind. (Ps. 22:18.)

Luke adds (23:44) that from midday to 3 p.m. 'the sun's light failed'. This was like an eclipse, but no eclipse is known, so perhaps a mighty cloud formation — the darkening of the sun of humanity through moon knowledge. Associated with it was a series of earthquakes, the first of which tore the veil of the temple (Matt. 27:51), revealing the Holy of Holies.

At this fourth stage of Christian mind-soul initiation one had to identify with every other being, with the whole earth, and with Christ as Spirit of the Earth. One has the world on one's conscience. Then one no longer connects the ego with the body, but carries that around like a block of wood, feeling, My body goes through the door. Though conscious of the occult powers latent in the body, one lives in a spiritual body. At length one sees oneself with the cross on one's back; the stigmata appear many times during meditation – the ordeal of blood – and inner vision arises of being nailed to the cross. One is thus initiated whilst within the physical body (List α). Modern Rosicrucian initiation replaces this by the development of Intuition, a universe-consciousness in which one becomes one, merges in love, with the spiritual Beings of the Hierarchies, a 'dwelling in God'. The stigmata are replaced by experience of Christ as Lord of Karma. Breathing, and life itself, must be made rhythmical by regular meditation, 'preparing the philosopher's stone' (a soft, trans-parent form of carbon) – the future body to be created through the larynx (p. 109) (List β).

19:25–30 *It Has Been Achieved*

25 But there stood by the cross of Jesus his mother, and his mother's sister Mary Clopas, and Mary Magdalene. **26** Jesus, seeing his mother and the disciple whom he loved standing by, says to his mother, Woman, behold your son. **27** Then he says to the disciple, Behold your mother. And from that hour the dis-ciple took her to his own.

28 After this, knowing that all has now been achieved, Jesus says – that the scripture might be completed – I thirst. **29** A vessel full of wine vinegar was set there, so putting a sponge full of vinegar round a hyssop, they brought it to his mouth. **30** So when Jesus took the vinegar he said, It has been achieved. And bowing his head, he delivered up the Spirit.

Since the mother's sister was called Mary, 'his mother' was not, though she clearly had been (Matt. 1:18). She had an exceptionally purified spiritual soul illumined by the Cosmic Ego, and was called in esoteric Christianity the Virgin Sophia (p. 26).

But there is a deeper meaning. Jesus instituted between his mother and John a new kind of fellowship based not on blood but on life ether, the 'living water' (4:14) which will organize life eternally. In the mysteries, 'mother' always meant something that needed to be inseminated on ascent to a higher level. The soul of Jesus of Nazareth—which as mother-soul of humanity had not incarnated before entering the Luke child—'was at the Baptism inseminated by the Holy Spirit (1:33), and gave rise to the entirely new Being of Jesus Christ' (3.10.13). This soul was thus 'the mother of Jesus'. The Christ-principle had first to be united with this etheric maternal element for John to penetrate consciously the cosmic mysteries of Christ from the sphere of Providence (beyond the zodiac). Now Jesus transfers these forces, with their power of Christian *katharsis*, to the beloved disciple, and thereby makes John 'the son of Sophia'. 'This enables him to write his Gospel in such a way that the divine wisdom, Sophia herself, is incarnated in it for the benefit of mankind. Thereby every soul may become receptive to the Holy Spirit' (4.7.09).

Death by crucifixion was barbarous, and normally took days. Jesus, already weak, had taken control by bowing his head, thus constricting the windpipe.

An archetype does not exist for what occurred on Golgotha. Only humans on earth experience death; all other beings experience only metamorphosis. Christ had to experience on behalf of the gods all that human beings experience in death. And 'the essential secret of death could be imparted only after it had been experienced on earth by a god, namely that Christ passed through it unchanged. All who know this can believe in the living Christ' (1.7.09).

We can share the death experience of Christ, and once this becomes a strong force he appears as risen Lord. This death was really an outpouring of all-prevailing cosmic love. Death is only the other side of birth. 'The deepest Christian experience of all is that human beings, through having gradually killed the seeds of life forces ever since our incarnations began, are responsible for the death on Golgotha. Only by knowing and realizing this, and by preparing for Christ to live again in our heart, can this be healed' (4.3.11). The soul must be able to have the Christ Triumphant before and within it, especially in the will.

At the fifth stage of Christian initiation – Mystic Death – the pupil feels that a black curtain obliterates the whole sense world. He plunges into the primal causes of evil, pain and sorrow – the descent into hell. Then it is as if the veil of the temple were 'rent in twain', and light and sound arise from the other side of existence. In contact with the inverse quality of things we begin to live again in a quite new world around us. We become a second person, the disciple, beside the lower self, the 'mother' (List α). The fifth stage of the Christian-Rosicrucian initiation seeks the Correspondence of Microcosm and Macrocosm; by intense meditation on bodily organs such as that at the root of the nose, the lungs, the inner organs, the whole physical body is transformed as foundation for the true 'I'. This leads to a loving relationship, wholly of spirit, to all things, to the cosmic situations through which we were created (List β).

19:31–37 Bone and Blood

31 Since it was Preparation, and so that the bodies might not remain on the Cross on the sabbath, for that sabbath was the great day, the Jews asked Pilate for their legs to be broken, and for them to be taken away. **32** So the soldiers came, and broke the legs of the first and of the other crucified with him; **33** but coming to Jesus, when they saw that he had already died, they did not break his legs; **34** but one of the soldiers pierced his side with a lance, and immediately there came out blood and water. **35** He who saw it has testified, and his testimony is true, and he knows that he speaks truly, that you too may believe. **36** For these things happened that the scripture might be fulfilled: A bone of him shall not be broken. **37** And again another scripture says: They shall look at him whom they pierced.

Christ had since the Baptism unique power over the bones of Jesus in a material sense (p. 27). The skeleton – the material expression of the archetypal human form – is an accurate symbol of death, whereas the Christ-impulse is the living force which transforms the whole physical kingdom, leading man upwards to what is spiritual. Bones must therefore be kept intact until mankind has awoken the inner force to spiritualize himself. Without this, we would have nothing to carry over to Jupiter. Had a bone been broken, an inferior force would have interfered with the power of Christ.

The loss of blood, the bearer of the ego, was of utmost future significance. 'Because his blood arose in Galilee from the greatest mix of nations (p. 25), that of Jesus was the sublimate of all human blood' (29.7.06). Because the figure of Christ towered over him, Jesus had to receive five wounds where one sufficed in the mysteries. The wounds are actually portals for the outflow of quite new etheric forces. This blood was chemically identical to all other, but spiritually, with the blood from the pierced side (which John specially emphasizes, v. 35) was mingled infinite love and forgiveness, the full power of the ego. 'From the sweat that fell as blood on the Mount of Olives until the wounds on Golgotha, this blood had to flow into the whole of humanity. Through the regenerative power of this blood, the excessive egoism in the blood of the old communities was cleansed. This cleansing of the egoistic 'I' from the blood *is* the Mystery of Golgotha' (1.4.07). Since then it lives in the ether of the earth, and can enter the ethereal bloodstream from heart to head (p. 58) of those who develop real understanding of the Christ-impulse. Thereby a communal self of humanity, the love for all men, and also sudden initiation such as that of Paul, became possible.

'At the moment when the blood flowed, Christ really did descend to the underworld, and appeared to the souls of those who had laden themselves with sin and guilt' (15.7.14). (To see how the earth suffered from their decaying bodies would otherwise have tormented their souls.) He made possible the mighty force of brotherhood, through which alone karma can be worked out on earth. Further earthquakes (Matt. 27:52) then 'opened tombs' — the so-called 'harrowing of hell'.

During this particularly deep darkness, Christ himself, the Sun Logos, flowed into the very being of the earth, making it his body; he was born as the Spirit of the Earth (which originally came to be through him — 1.b). This fundamentally transformed the earth aura, such that a golden star appeared in the blue aura in the east over against the reddish-yellow glimmering in the west. 'This astral light will gradually become etheric light and then physical light, so that the earth will gradually become able to reunite with the sun and itself become a sun. The same astral force (not subject to death) also radiates into the etheric bodies of human beings who understand Christ — this was called the Holy Spirit. It too streams back into space, creating a spiritual sphere encircling the earth that will develop into a planet' (6.7.09).

The flowing of 'blood and water' points to the separation of astral and etheric bodies whilst yet on the cross. Both bodies are now multiplied in the spiritual world like a grain of seed, the astral retaining the copy of the human ego of Jesus (p. 143), now enhanced by all the effects of the Christ Ego.

19:38–42 *Deposition and Entombment*

38 Now after this Joseph of Arimathea, a disciple of Jesus but secretly for fear of the Jews, asked Pilate if he might take the body of Jesus; and Pilate allowed it. So he came and took his body away. **39** Nicodemus also, who came to him at first by night, came bringing a mixture of myrrh and aloes, about 75lbs. **40** They took the body of Jesus, and bound it in linen sheets with the spices, as is the burial custom of the Jews. **41** Now in the place where he was crucified was a garden, and in the garden a new tomb in which no one had ever yet been put. **42** So because of the Jewish Preparation, as the tomb was near, they laid Jesus there.

The physical body needs to be considered from the two aspects of form and substance. The physical human form is a work of the gods, originated on Saturn, shaped further on Sun and Moon, and perfected on Earth by the Spirits of Form (Elohim), but corrupted by Lucifer at the Fall. It is a transparent shape comprising physical forces of the nature of concepts, which holds the materials together during life and is known as the 'phantom'. As a result of the Baptism the phantom of Jesus had been released from all materials except the soluble salts (p. 18). For three years Christ lived in and worked on this body, so that when it was nailed to the cross the corruption by Lucifer had been made good (p. 87). 'This phantom, a spiritual body visible only super-sensibly, was thus intact, free, and unaffected by the material wounds' (12.10.11).

When the body of Jesus was laid in the grave, this phantom was carried by Christ right to the heart of the earth (Matt. 12:40). The ordinary human form is fragmented in the eighth sphere, but this one can instead multiply itself like a living cell, and impart itself to anyone who makes the necessary connection with Christ. It is this perfect phantom of Jesus which thus rises again redeemed, resurrected by Christ with forces for the future of humanity, which is known by Paul as the 'incorruptible body' or 'second Adam' (1 Cor. 15:42f.). 'Consciousness of the eternal 'I' results only from being reflected by this physical phantom, so this 'I' was thus literally rescued from loss' (11.10.11). Without this living form of the bony system which conquers death in a physical sense, human evolution would have been irretrievably lost. What is most important is not what Christ taught but what he gave—an imperishable body.

Substance is the result of the Fall. The substance of Jesus had already been anointed on the feet (12:3) and later on the head (Mark 14:3) with spikenard. Then he had been given vinegar, which is acidic (v. 29). When the body was taken down, the parts were still coherent, held together only by the power of the macrocosmic Christ, but disconnected from the phantom. Now it was wrapped in great quantities of myrrh, which worked quite differently from usual, so that the material parts quickly volati-lized and passed into the elements. The inner life that in the mysteries had been awakened on the astral plane was thus translated down to the physical plane.

According to tradition Joseph had collected the blood from the wounds of Jesus Christ, the expression and copy of his Ego, in the chalice called the Grail. Joseph was quickly imprisoned, but was freed by a vision of Christ, fled to the west, and originated the Grail stream. Whoever knows the mystery of the Holy Grail knows that from the wood of the cross springs living, budding life, the inmost self, symbolized by the roses on the dark wood. Nicodemus had been taught by Jesus of rebirth in the spirit (3:7) and spoken up for him (7:50).

The Resurrection

20:1–10 The Empty Tomb

1 On the first day after the sabbath, Mary Magdalene comes to the tomb early, while it was still dark, and sees that the stone had been taken from the tomb. **2** So she runs and comes to Simon Peter and the other disciple whom Jesus loved, and says to them, They took the Lord out of the tomb, and we do not know where they put him. **3** So Peter and the other disciple went out and came to the tomb. **4** The two ran together; and the other disciple ran in front, faster than Peter, and came first to the tomb; **5** and stooping, he catches sight of the sheets lying there but did not enter. **6** So Simon Peter comes following him and entered the tomb; and he sees the sheets lying, **7** and the kerchief that was on his head not lying with the sheets but apart, wrapped up in one place. **8** Then the other disciple who came first to the tomb also went in, and he perceived and believed; **9** for they did not yet know the scripture that he was to rise again from the dead. **10** So the disciples went away again to themselves.

'Early on the Sunday morning another shock (Matt. 28:2) wrenched away the stone covering the tomb of Jesus, a fissure opened, and what remained of the corpse was received into it. Further tremors then closed the fissure' (2.10.13) (said to have been visible in the Holy Sepulchre before it was covered with marble). When Mary Magdalene arrived early with other women—'we' (v. 2) includes Mary Clopas (Matt. 28:1), Salome (Mark 16:1) and Joanna (Luke 24:10)—she assumed that the body had been stolen, though the grave sheets and kerchief (tossed about by the shock waves and an associated whirlwind) would have shown the contrary. Matthew adds (27:66) that guards had been placed, but they were bribed to lie that the body had indeed been stolen. This is all described in terms of ordinary sense experiences.

Not only is the earth permeated with the Spirit of Christ even to the minutest particle, but also in the very laws of chemistry and physics. In future will be taught : 'I will remain with you unto the end of the earth' (Matt. 28:20). 'Went away to themselves' surely means entering meditation on such strange events.

The sixth stage of Christian mind-soul initiation, which began with the entombment, union with the earth, leads to the experience of Resurrection, becoming a planetary spirit within a planetary life united with the deepest soul of the planet, that of Christ. The pupil becomes a 'sun hero', who can depart from his path as little as the sun itself from the path to becoming a new sun. He now understands the whole post-Atlantean epoch (List α). In the modern spiritual soul initiation, when life spirit has been extensively developed for a whole race, its power emerges — this is the 'entombment'. Freed from the physical brain, the initiate lives into all creation, and perceives the Creator behind it, in deep calm contemplation — one must leave oneself behind. This is the stage of Living with the Macrocosm (List β).

20:11–18 Mary Magdalene

11 But Mary stood outside the tomb, weeping. As she wept, she bent down into the tomb, **12** and beholds two angels in white sitting one at the head and one at the feet where the body of Jesus had lain. **13** They say to her, Woman, why do you weep? She says, They took my Lord, and I do not know where they put him. **14** Saying this, she turned back and beholds Jesus standing, and did not know that it was Jesus. **15** Jesus says to her, Woman, why do you weep? Whom do you seek? She, thinking that it is the gardener, says to him, Sir, if you carried him away, tell me where you put him, and I will take him. **16** Jesus says to her, Mary. Turning, She says to him in Hebrew, Rabboni (which means Teacher). **17** Jesus says to her, Do not touch me, for I have not yet risen to the Father; but go to my brothers and tell them that I am rising to my Father and your Father, my God and your God. **18** Mary Magdalene comes to the disciples, declaring, I have seen the Lord; and these things that he said to her.

Mary Magdalene had a purified sentient soul (seven demons had come out of her—Luke 8:2), and her experiences at the anointment and the crucifixion had developed powerful inner forces of clairvoyance. She first had a vision (not then uncommon) of the spiritual forms of the etheric and astral bodies, always visible for a time when a corpse is present. 'She had hallowed her physical body so far that she alone of humans could take it to the fixed star heaven' (20.11.07).

The etheric body of Jesus of Nazareth bore all his unique memories to the Akashic Record, which forms in the Saturn sphere, the realm of 'my Father and your Father'. 'It is through this alone that the Gospels can be researched in their true original form' (8.10.11). An etheric body takes three days to expand to the cosmos, and this especially must not be distorted by touch (though Matt. 28:9 says the disciples took hold of his feet). Although this is 'the third day', only 39 hours have passed since Friday 3 p.m.

What Mary and the others saw clairvoyantly, including Paul, was the newly risen phantom. Since this phantom was no longer weighed down by physical substance Mary could not recognize it; but when the sacred force of the Word echoed in her heart, turned her consciousness (inwards) and kindled her memory, she did.

'The Nathan soul of Jesus was retained by Christ as his soul sheath, through which he continues to work' (p. 143) (1.1.13).

20:19–31 The Closed Room

19 During the early evening of that day, the first of the week, the doors where the disciples were having been shut because of fear of the Jews, Jesus came and stood in the midst and says to them, Peace to you. **20** Saying this, he showed them both his hands and his side. The disciples rejoiced on beholding the Lord. **21** Jesus said to them again, Peace to you; as the Father has sent me, I also send you. **22** Saying this he drew breath and says to them, Receive Holy Spirit. **23** Of whomsoever you forgive the sins, they have been forgiven; of whomsoever you hold, they have been held. **24** But Thomas, one of the Twelve called Twin, was not with them when Jesus came. **25** So the other disciples said to him, We have seen the Lord. But he said, unless I behold in his hands the mark of the nails, and put my finger into the place of the nails and put my hand into his side, I will not believe.

26 After eight days his disciples were again within, and Thomas with them. The doors having been shut, Jesus comes, and stood in the midst and said, Peace to you. **27** Then he says to Thomas, Bring your finger here, and behold my hands, and bring your hand and put it into my side, and be not faithless but faithful. **28** Thomas replied, My Lord and my God. **29** Jesus says to him, Have you believed because you have seen me? Blessed are those who do not behold, and yet believe. **30** And Jesus did many other signs before the disciples which are not written in this book. **31** But these have been written that you may believe that Jesus is the Christ the Son of God, and that, believing, you may have life in his name.

This is a different inner experience ('in the midst') involving the rhythmic system, a communal meditation behind closed doors. The etheric element that Christ had used to restore the phantom consisted of 'forces reaching into the future as far as Jupiter evolution, and bearing the promised forces of eternal life (3:15 etc.). It gave new life to the vast bodily tableau, and was permeated by the etherized blood that bore the etheric scars of the wounds' (10.2.14). Through the power of Christ it was able to condense for Imagination to the point of physical visibility as the Risen Christ. (Luke 24:39: I am myself). 'This etheric body is the only one to appear in the physical world as a human body appears, and in many places at once' (1.10.11). Only through the disciples being joined in harmonious companionship with Christ could they see him in a perfect phantom of head and breast, rescued from the primal human form which had been drained of blood and taken into the earth.

Only because the Apostles received the Holy Spirit could they receive the Fullness of the living Word at Whitsun. But only John, as an initiate, can recognize the Spirit consciously through the breath. The others, still in shock and half asleep, must wait until it is given by the Father not only with breath/air but also with fire, the outpouring of human love (Acts 2:1). (It had previously been given in the mysteries, but only when out of the body.) The gift through the breath must be recognized as an entirely new beginning (1.1, Gen. 2:7). 'I send you' (v. 21) inaugurates the Christian mission, for which Holy Spirit is given. This is a clear answer to the medieval *Filioque* dispute.

Eight days later the Risen One cannot be damaged by touch. 'In the new part of the etheric body with which Christ clothed himself were especially dense places corresponding to the wounds' (9.1.12). The sense experience of 'doubting' Thomas is so powerful that he can believe, which is an inner clairvoyant power. It is a meeting with Christ in the very depths of soul, in which the spirit is brought to life as Life Spirit. The last verse is often regarded as the original end of the Gospel, but a further progression of consciousness is yet to come.

The meeting on the road to Emmaus (Luke 24:13f.) in which Christ walks beside two disciples and dissolves food is an experience of his etheric body. And Paul speaks (1 Cor. 15:6) of his appearing to 'more than 500 at the same time'. This is the beginning of Christ's expansion into space, where his higher principles are to be found 'on the clouds of heaven' (Matt. 26:64). 'After the Resurrection Christ gave his disciples an esoteric schooling, with many profound details (Acts 1:3). But these were rejected in AD 869 because the church wanted to be rid of anything cosmic' (13.9.24).

21:1–14 Fish for Breakfast

1 After this Jesus revealed himself again to the disciples by the sea of Tiberias, and in this way. 2 Simon Peter, Thomas the Twin, Nathanael from Cana in Galilee, the sons of Zebedee and two others of his disciples were together. 3 Simon Peter says to them, I'm going fishing. They say, we're coming with you too. They went out and embarked on the boat, and that night caught nothing. 4 But in the early morning Jesus stood into the shore; but

the disciples did not know that it was Jesus. **5** So Jesus says to them, Children, have you any fish? They answered, No. **6** So he said, Cast the net to the right of the boat, and you will find some. So they cast, and were no longer able to haul it in for the multitude of fish. **7** That disciple whom Jesus loved says to Peter, It is the Lord. So Simon Peter, hearing that it was the Lord, tied his garment round him, for he was stripped, and threw himself into the sea; **8** but the other disciples come in the boat, dragging the net of fish, for they were not far from land, about a hundred yards. **9** When they landed they see a charcoal fire, and fish lying on it, and bread. **10** Jesus says, Bring some of the fish you have just caught. **11** Simon Peter went and dragged the net to land full of large fish, a hundred and fifty three; and although there were so many, the net was not torn. **12** Jesus says, Come and have breakfast. None of the disciples ventured to ask him, Who are you? Knowing that it was the Lord. **13** Jesus comes and takes the bread and gives it to them, and likewise the fish. **14** This was now the third time that Jesus was revealed to the disciples, raised from the dead.

This is a different experience again, involving the metabolic-limb system, economic life; through seven people we are first led back to everyday life. The scene is on John's route to Patmos. Jesus now appears ('into' — *eis* — suggests an apparition) in a purely practical way, advising where to cast, and providing fire and food for those who have worked all night (cf. Luke 5:4f.). Again it is the etheric body of Christ that is seen.

Although the disciples knew that they had been with Jesus as a spiritual figure, only John was awake enough to recognize him in his new form. They saw that Jesus had instructed them, but could not understand it. Hence he spoke to them again as children (cf. 13:33) rather than as brothers (20:17).

The fish remind us of the new age of Pisces and the feeding of the five thousand (6:11); but giving thanks is now conspicuously omitted. Christ is not only himself the Bread of Life (6:35) but now also 'on the land', becoming the Spirit of the Earth, the substance of which is thereby already sanctified. The fish became an early symbol for Christianity, with disciples seen as fishers of men. Significantly it is John who recognizes the Lord, but Peter who drags in the fish.

The number 153 is triangular, the sum of all integers up to 17. In Hebrew 153 is gematria for 'ages to come'. 'Most probably it refers to the 17 ages remaining until the end of the physical earth in warmth (7 Trumpets, 7 Seals plus the 5th, 6th and 7th post-Atlantean ages)' (undated). That is the end of the physical Stage of Form, when 'heaven and earth shall pass away, but my Word shall not pass away' (Mark 13:31). John developed this in his Apocalypse (Rev. 11:15f.).

21:15–25 The Two Streams

15 When they had breakfasted, Jesus says to Simon Peter, Simon son of John, do you Love me more than these? He says, Yes, Lord, you know that I love you. So he says, Feed my lambs. **16** He says for a second time, Simon son of John, do you Love me? He says, Yes, Lord, you know that I love you. He says, Tend my little sheep. **17** He says the third time, Simon son of John, do you love me? Peter was grieved that he said the third time, Do you love me, and said, Lord, you know all, you Know that I love you; Jesus says to him, Feed my little sheep. **18** Truly I tell you, when you were younger you girded yourself and walked where you wished; but when you grow old, you will stretch out your hands, and another will gird you and will carry you where you do not wish. **19** This he said, signifying by what death he will glorify God. And saying this, he tells him, Follow me.

20 Turning, Peter sees following them the disciple whom Jesus Loved, who also at the supper leaned on his breast and said, Lord, who is betraying you? **21** So, seeing him, Peter says to Jesus, what of him? **22** Jesus says to him, If I wish him to abide until I come, what is that to you? You follow me! **23** Consequently this word spread to the brothers, that that disciple does not die; but Jesus did not say that he does not die, but: If I wish him to abide until I come, what is that to you?

24 This is the disciple who bears witness to these things and has written them, and we Know that his witness is true. **25** There are also many other things which Jesus did, which if they were written separately, I think the world itself would not contain the books written.

John finally brings into the open the polarity between Peter, the oldest and leading disciple, and himself, the young initiate. This began with their seating at the Last Supper, through Peter's denial and John's presence at the Crucifixion, the race to the tomb, and John's greater insight (v. 7). Now Jesus twice asks in terms of *agape*, the term used in 'the beloved disciple'. Peter replies in terms of *philein* – he is devoted to Jesus, but after his threefold denial does not feel able to claim 'as I (Jesus) love you' (13:34). When the third time Jesus asks in terms of *philein*, Peter can affirm it. This threefold affirmation redeems his denial, and his eventual martyrdom is fully respected.

Peter receives two instructions, to 'feed/tend my lambs/ sheep' and to 'follow me'. He fulfilled the first by founding the church, which tended and gave spiritual nourishment to many, and the second by his death. But the work of the beloved disciple is to be quite independent – 'what is that to you?' He is to 'abide until I come'. His immediate task (v. 24) is clearly to write an esoteric gospel, for which he is uniquely qualified. In it he expresses a different relationship to the sheep (10:9): 'to lead them in and out to find pasture'. This has been practised in such movements as the Grail stream, the original Rosicrucians, and now in anthroposophy, but in our time only reaches the pre- liminary stage of Appearing; it must abide until the Second Coming in the seventh age for full flowering of the *parousia*.

'The disciples saw Christ over and over again (v. 25), more often than the Bible records; but after 40 days their vision lost its power' (9.5.23). 'For the "I" to arise in full, clear consciousness while Christ dwelt still within the individual, it was necessary for him to pass away to the astral plane' (26.6.05), thus vanishing from actual sight. This is expressed as the Ascension (Mark 16:19, Acts 1:9). Ascension and the outpouring of spirit at Whitsun may be compared with our entering the world of spirit after we die.

The seventh stage of the Christian mind-soul initiation is also called Ascension, which cannot be described in words. What ascends is the pure phantom or 'incorruptible body', not of course the corpse. It represents complete absorption into the spiritual world, bringing the power to heal but also to cause disease (List α). In the Rosicrucian initiation for the present age, this stage is called Divine Bliss or Godliness, a feeling of blessedness which may only be added in utterly selfless service to humanity. It foreshadows the ultimate reunion of earth and sun in the next Stage of Form (List β).

Epilogue

During the 2000 years since the Gospel was written, the evolution of humanity has progressed. 'Even the disciples were unable to understand Christ, right up to their deaths. Only in the third century were they sufficiently mature to inspire the Church Fathers from the life after death, but the difficulty of inspiring mankind increased, until in 869 the Spirit was denied' (13.10.18).

The promise by Jesus Christ to send the Holy Spirit (14:16) was renewed with the descent of the Cosmic Intelligence, the development of widespread individual thinking, between the seventh and twelfth centuries, centred in the ninth. This made possible the development of the consciousness soul (spiritual soul) from the fifteenth century.

Between the sixth and ninth centuries, copies of the etheric body of Jesus were incorporated in leading Christian individuals such as Augustine or Patrick. From the eleventh to the fifteenth centuries copies of his astral body were incorporated in such people as Francis of Assisi or Elizabeth of Thüringia. And in the fourteenth to seventeenth centuries were incorporated in the German mystics copies of the Jesus ego, heightened by the Christ event (16.5.09).

But the materialism of the nineteenth century was such that the astral light of Jesus which had previously shone in certain human souls was extinguished (2.5.13). Christ now builds for himself new sheaths through human wonder, compassion and conscience.

Then at the end of the nineteenth century, the 5000 years of Kali Yuga, the dark age, was completed, and a new age of light began. Again the Nathan soul of Jesus participates directly in the etheric advent of Christ in our time, as expressed for instance by Theodora in the first Mystery Play. And the path of anthroposophy opens.

'There is nothing to prevent a person who comes to grasp how Christ's own development progresses, and with it how certain human capacities develop, from participating when they pass through death in the event of Damascus. For death actually manifests now as an initial shining forth of Christ into the world of humanity' (5.12.11). But it only becomes possible for Christ to appear before the soul when through human organology (p. 71) we can extend our vision to cosmic man, for as cosmic man he descended from the sun.

'Today we must say, seek for the Spirit that reveals itself in the Word, for the Spirit *is* with God, and the Spirit *is* a God' (2.11.19). Christ must be found through the Holy Spirit, the descended Cosmic Intelligence (i.e. be understood). 'We have progressed so far in evolution that the first words of the Gospel may now be set forth thus:

> In the primal origin is the Thought
> And the Thought is with God
> And a godlike Being is the Thought
> In it is Life
> And the Life shall become the Light of my ego,
> And the Divine Thought shine into my ego
> That the darkness of my ego may grasp the Thought Divine.

'We now have to prepare for the introduction of the Christ-impulse into the human capacity of memory, so that in the sixth age it may reach back over former incarnations' (7.3.14). 'In the seventh age an evangelist will have to say that the flesh becomes Word' (21.9.11). 'And one day the Word will become God' (12.4.17).

Bibliography

(Warning: all references before 1908 are from notes taken by participants.)

From	To	CW	
29.5.05		93	*The Temple Legend*
26.6.05			Typescript Z 211 On the Gospel of St John (Berlin)
9.10.05	3.11.05	93a	*Foundations of Esotericism*
13.2.06	30.7.06	97	*The Christian Mystery*
19.2.06		94	*The Gospel of St John* (Berlin)
28.10.06	6.11.06	94	*Kosmogonie. Das Johannes Evangelium* (Munich)
2.12.06	17.3.07	97	*The Christian Mystery*
21.3.07			*Rosicrucianism Renewed*
25.3.07	1.4.07	96	*Festivals of the Seasons/Original Impulses for the Science of the Spirit/Christian Mystery*
20.11.07	22.11.07	100	Typescript EN50. Notes on St John's Gospel (Basel)
20.5.08	30.5.08	103	*The Gospel of St John* (Hamburg)
24.6.08	30.6.08		*The Apocalypse of St John*
6.8.08		105	*Universe, Earth and Man*
15.2.09		109	*Christianity in the Evolution of Mankind/The Principle of Spiritual Economy*
22.3.09		107	*The Deed of Christ*
10.4.09		109	*Festivals of the Seasons/Easter/The Principle of Spiritual Economy*
18.4.09		110	*Spiritual Hierarchies and their Physical Work*
16.5.09		104a	*Reading the Pictures of the Apocalypse*
27.5.09			*Esoteric Lessons 1904–1909*
1.7.09	7.7.09	112	*The Gospel of St John and its Relation to other Gospels* (Kassel)
29.8.09		113	*The East in the Light of the West*
20.9.09		114	*The Gospel of St Luke/According to Luke*
8.2.10		116	*The Christ Impulse and the Development of Ego-Consciousness*
1.9.10	11.9.10	123	*The Gospel of St Matthew*

9.5.23		349	*From Limestone to Lucifer*
2.12.23		232	*Mystery Knowledge and Mystery Centres/ Mystery Centres*
15.2.24			Esoteric Lessons, School of Spiritual Science
16.6.24		239	*Agriculture Course*
21.8.24	22.8.24	243	*True and False Paths in Spiritual Investigation*
13.9.24		346	*Book of Revelation and the Work of the Priest*
28.9.24		238	*The Last Address/Karmic Relationships Vol. IV*
undated			Typescript *c.* 1908
CMF		8	*Christianity as Mystical Fact*

List α

	26.2.06	94	*The Gospel of St John* (Berlin)
	1.6.06	94	*An Esoteric Cosmology*
Various	1906/7	97	*The Christian Mystery*
	3.9.06	95	*At the Gates/Founding a Science/Self-Transformation*
	6.6.07	99	*Theosophy of the Rosicrucians*
	30.5.08	103	*The Gospel of St John* (Hamburg)
	7.7.09	112	*The Gospel of St John and its Relation to the Other Gospels* (Kassel)

List β

	4.9.06	95	*At the Gates of Spiritual Science/Founding a Science of the Spirit/Self-Transformation*
Various	1906/7	97	*The Christian Mystery*
	21.10.06	96	*Original Impulses for the Science of the Spirit/ Esoteric Development*
	6.6.07	99	*Theosophy of the Rosicrucians/Rosicrucian Wisdom*
	12.8.08	105	*Universe Earth and Man/Love and its Meaning in the World*
		10	*Knowledge of the Higher Worlds*
		13	*Occult Science/Esoteric Science*